my point...
and I do
have one

ELLEN DEGENERES

my point...
and I do
have one

BANTAM BOOKS
New York Toronto London Sydney Auckland

MY POINT . . . AND I DO HAVE ONE
A Bantam Book

PUBLISHING HISTORY
Bantam hardcover edition published October 1995
Bantam mass market edition published October 1996
Bantam trade paperback edition / October 2007

Published by Bantam Dell
A Division of Random House, Inc.
New York, New York

BOOK DESIGN BY DONNA SINISGALLI

Bantam Books and the rooster colophon are registered trademarks of Random House, Inc.

Library of Congress Catalog Card Number: 95-34084

ISBN 978-0-553-38422-2

Printed in the United States of America
Published simultaneously in Canada

www.bantamdell.com

BVG   10 9 8 7

Table O'Contents

Introduction to the Paperback Edition   ix

A Note from the Author   xi

Thanks for No Memory   1

A Letter to My Friend
or
A Frog in a Sombrero Does Not a Party Make   13

Daily Affirmations
or
A Cup of Pudding a Day Is the Way to Stay O.K.   19

Ellen DeGeneres: Road Warrior
or
Sometimes You Need a Map,
Sometimes You Need a Globe,
Sometimes You Need a Map and a Globe—
but Not Very Often   25

The Plane Truth
or
Dem Ain't Goobers, Dem's Peanuts!   37

Ellen's New Hobby   47

Ellenvision   57

I Went to a Psychic
or
Baloney Is Just Salami with an Inferiority Complex   63

How to Explain Sex to a Child
or
Where There's a Corn Chip,
There's Bound to Be Hot Sauce   71

In the Kitchen with Ellen
or
As Tasty as Poison and Just as Deadly   79

Things That Sound Like a Good Idea at First,
but Really Aren't   87

Ellen DeGeneres Is a Man!
or
Ellen DeGeneres Is a Man!   91

Chapter 13   99

Chapter 14   103

The Scariest Thing   107

The Time Ellen DeGeneres Had an Emergency!   117

One Step Closer to God
or
One Step Back,
You Do the Hokey-Pokey
and You Turn Yourself Around   125

The Ellie-Gellie   133

Things to Do if You're Stuck in an Elevator to Help
You Pass the Time   139

Ellen's Wild Kingdom
or
You Can Put High Heels on a Poodle,
but That Won't Make It a Hooker   143

Ask Ellen
or
It Might Look Like Honey,
It Might Taste Like Honey,
and Bless My Corns,
It Might Even Be Honey   155

Crazy Superstitions That Really Work!   165

The Benefits of Being a Celebrity
By Ellen DeGeneres, Big Enormous Star   169

Your Own Fantasy Conversation with Ellen
DeGeneres   175

Experiments in Human Behavior   185

Ellen's Sure-Fire Cures for the
Things That Ail Ye   199

The Last Chapter   207

Acknowledgments

I wish to thank a few people for their support and love, which are two of the most important things in my life: Betty DeGeneres, Elliott DeGeneres (or Mom and Dad), Vance DeGeneres, Arthur Imparato, Rob Weisbach, Alex Herschlag, Sue Rose, Lisa Phillips, J. J. Harris, Jeremy Zimmer, Ted Harbert, Stu Bloomberg, Renee Kurtz, Michael Eisner, Rich Frank, Dean Valentine, Jan Nash, Karen Kawahara, and Eric Bilardi. And all of the people who come up to me on the street and tell me nice things. Thank you.

A New Introduction to the Trade Paperback Edition

Check it out! It's a brand-new book from me, the author, Ellen DeGeneres.

Well, the words aren't new, but the picture is and these words here are. Not that they're new words—like they've never been used before; just that they've never been used in this book before.

Well, that's not true either. I'm sure all of these words do appear in the first edition in some form or another, but not in this exact order. They may have been used in this exact order in some other book that I've never read, so I don't know that I'm plagiarizing, if in fact I am. If that is the case, I apologize to that author. I know these words were hard to string together and I'm sure you don't want someone else taking credit for your work.

Although I doubt you would have put in that apology part, so I feel pretty good about claiming this as my own. Also, if you did already write this, then you wrote that you were Ellen DeGeneres, which means you're an impostor! How dare you accuse me when you're the one who's the criminal! Expect a call from my lawyer.

As for the rest of you, please enjoy this new version of my old book.

A Note from the Author

Hello and welcome to my book (and now yours). Thank you for your interest in my thoughts, my words of wisdom, and my recipe for French toast. Throughout the year it took me to write this, I wrote in solitude, recording my thoughts as they came to me, digging up old memories, pouring out my heart and soul. Then, at the end of the process, I hoped and prayed to God that there were a few people out there who would enjoy it.

As you may have noticed, my mind does not work the same as most. That is to say, I'm sort of, well—different—and yet it seems to have worked for me. So as you read this, I hope it does what I intended it to do when I decided to write it. I hope it entertains you, inspires you, makes you laugh, makes you think, makes you smile, makes you feel better about yourself, makes you more aware of your feelings, makes you love your brothers and sisters, makes you more successful in life, makes you wealthier, makes you exercise more, makes you eat healthier, makes you stop smoking, makes you taller, thinner, more beautiful, more fluent in Spanish! Or at least makes you not regret buying it.

Ellen DeGeneres
June 1995

thanks for no memory

....

That's not my life...

Who am I? How did I get to be me? If I wasn't me, who would I be? How can you mend a broken heart? These are all good questions. Well, almost all good questions—I'm pretty sure the last one is just a Bee Gees song.

Anyway, what I'm trying to say is who I am now is what I was then, plus all the stuff in between, minus a few years during the seventies. Actually, that might not be what I'm trying to say. Here's what I really mean: When you start to write a book, you begin at the beginning; when you start to examine your life, you begin with childhood.

I try to work on my memory. A few things come back to me when I concentrate. Like, I'm now pretty sure I had parents. I have these two old people who are my parents now, and they say they were also my parents then. I'm thirty-six. I *was* a little girl. I know because my parents say I was.

I was born in Jefferson Parish, Louisiana, at Ochsner Hospital, January 26, 1958. I lived in a house on Haring Road in Metairie until I was . . . oh, let's say eight or nine—maybe ten . . . could've been seven or six, I don't know.

I don't think I remember my first memory. Actually, I suppose I would have to remember my first memory. If I didn't remember my first memory, then it couldn't in all honesty be my first memory. It could, however, be the first thing that I forgot. Do I recall the first thing that I forgot? I don't remember. Maybe.

I am amazed when people tell me that they remember things like lying in their cribs or getting their diapers changed (these are things they remember doing as infants not as adults —that would be an entirely different story and probably not a very pleasant one). Some people even remember learning how to walk, which I find especially surprising since I just barely remember learning how to drive.

Sometimes my lack of memory (or, to put a positive spin on it, my surplus of forgetfulness) worries me, especially since it's not limited to my early childhood. I don't remember huge portions of my life. Maybe something big (i.e., an anvil or France) fell on my head and gave me a slight form of amnesia. Maybe a lot of things have fallen on my head. I just don't know.

My parents have tried to help me out, but they remember even less about me than I do. They hardly took any pictures of me. But my brother—who was four years older than me (and still is, as a matter of fact)—they took so many pictures of him that you can flip through his photos and it's like one of those animation books; it looks like a movie where he's walking and riding a tricycle and running around. They must have taken a picture of him every ten seconds.

After four years of that, my parents must have gotten tired. I came along and they said, "We don't have to take any pictures. We'll remember." But they don't. It was ridiculous. There were statues of my brother around the house, but nothing of me. They tried to fool me and show me pictures they said were of me. But I'd say, "That's not me. Those are pictures you cut out of a magazine. I know, because I'm neither Elizabeth Taylor nor a member of England's royal family."

So I decided to do something to fill in these great gaps in my memory. I set out to interview people who knew me through various stages of my life. Most of those I interviewed didn't look familiar, but I'm sure they were telling me the truth. Otherwise they wouldn't have answered the ads or accepted the money I gave them. What follows are the transcripts of some of those interviews.

....

My Investigation Notes:

I was born, bred, and lightly sautéed in and around New Orleans, a city steeped in tradition and marinated in history. During those formative years, a trusted family friend and neighbor was Miss Selma Clanque (pronounced Klan-kay), a woman who earned her living making decorative jewelry out of crawdads.

I interviewed Miss Selma, now a feisty spitfire in her early seventies, on the fire escape of her apartment (which she insisted we call a lanai). Throughout, she chain-smoked clove cigarettes and drank a mixture of Ovaltine and vodka, a cocktail she calls chocolate thunder.

What do you remember most about me as a baby?
You were fat. Oh lordy, were you fat! You didn't walk for the longest time, 'cause you were so fat. They just rolled you wherever they wanted you to go.

Anything besides that?
I think your parents just kept feeding you. They were happy you weren't walking. They already had your brother, a very handsome boy—no fat on him—so they figured, might as well let you take your time.

Do you remember anything not having to do with my being fat?
Well . . . you had a big old head, too, and not a lick of hair on it. Bless my corns, you were one ugly baby. Now you know that Miss Selma Clanque's mother didn't raise her to say nothing mean about no one. But your mama dressed you in the most hideous clothes—flowery frocks and bonnets and the like. Now when you've got a bone ugly child, you don't want to bring more attention to it. Am I right?

Let's move on. Do you have any memories of me from when I was in grade school?
I recall you coming home all upset because there was a cloak-room in your class and you didn't own a cloak. In fact, none of the little boys or girls had a cloak. I don't think any of them even knew what a cloak was. For some reason this scared you.

Do you remember my being good at anything?
You would nap better than anybody else, and your parents would brag on you being good at recess. You were quite a good tetherball player, probably because you were so aggressive.

I remember tetherball. A ball would be attached to a pole by a rope and you'd try to whack the ball hard enough to wrap the rope around the pole. It was violent. You'd either hurt your hand on the metal thingee holding the rope and ball together or you'd be on defense, standing in front of the ball, and get hit in the face. Somebody would always end up crying.
Well, crying's good. It prepares you for life. The more often I see children crying, the more often I think, "That's gonna be a healthy adult." That's what life is all about. There's a lot of crying involved. So you'd better cry now and get used to it.

Well, it's nice to know that I was good at something.
Oh my, yes! You were so good at tetherball that I bet someone $100 cash that you would become a professional tetherball player.

I guess you had to pay up?
Why? You ain't dead yet. There's still time. Everybody's always trying to get Miss Selma Clanque to give them $100, just like it grew on trees. Look at me, I ain't Rockefeller, am I?

No, you're not. Thanks for the time. I've got to go.

I moved to Atlanta, Texas, in my second year of high school. When Columbus came to the New World, he thought he was in India so he referred to the people he met as Indians. When the first settlers came to Texas, they thought they were in Georgia, so they called the place Atlanta. It was a culture shock moving from New Orleans (The French Quarter, Jazz, great restaurants) to such a small town as Atlanta (Dairy Queen). So, I learned a different way of life.

My high school guidance counselor in Atlanta was Mr. Bowden Lamar, a man rumored to have a wonderfully infectious laugh; rumored, because no one living had actually ever heard him laugh. We spoke in his office at Atlanta High where, though he appeared to be somewhere in his early hundreds, he still doles out advice as a guidance counselor.

Mr. Lamar, was I a good student here?
Well, the teachers here remember you very fondly. They all say you were very bright.

Why, thank you. I guess that's . . .
But they're just saying that because you're famous now. I know because I've seen your records.

What do those records say?
That the only reason you passed any class was because your teachers gave you very broad clues. For instance, if the answer to a question was Thomas Jefferson, your teacher would say, "The answer to that rhymes with Bhomas Hefferson." If you still couldn't guess, she'd start singing, "Movin' on up, to the East Side. We finally got a piece of the pie."

The theme from "The Jeffersons"?
Exactly. Sooner or later—usually later—you'd end up getting the answer.

Was I good at anything?
Athletics, I suppose. You were on the tennis team. And you started the girls golf team. You were the only one on the team, playing every day by yourself. You would whack the ball very aggressively then acknowledge the applause of a crowd that only existed in your mind. Very strange and more than slightly disturbing.

Do you remember what I looked like?
Well, you were a little hefty. Yup, you were a little hefty girl who'd drive to school each day in a canary yellow Vega. But then again, everybody here is a little hefty. That's because the only kind of food you can get around here is chicken-fried. Chicken-fried steak, chicken-fried broccoli, chicken-fried sushi, chicken-fried whatever.

What sort of career do your records say I was best suited for?
Let me see. Oh here it is. "Ellen DeGeneres might be good at making caramel candies of some kind, either chewy or hard. Not the wrapping, just the candy."

Just one last question. How come this school didn't have a drama department?
Oh, we had a drama department. We all just thought it was best for everybody involved that you never knew about it. Whenever we wanted to put on a play, we'd just send you golfing somewhere. Ha, ha, it's kind of funny, isn't it?

Yeah, hilarious.

As soon as I graduated from high school, I moved back to New Orleans. I had no plans to go to college and no idea what I was going to do, but I don't remember caring either. After all, it was the 1970s, and the country was tapping its platform shoes to the sounds of K.C. and the Sunshine Band.

I worked at a series of places including a restaurant (where I shucked oysters) and a law firm (where I shucked lawyers). A friend of mine during that time was Rita Bangs, an aspiring coffee importer. I interviewed Rita at a Renaissance Faire called "Ye Olden Dress Up in Funny Clothes Thymes" where she was employed as a wench.

When you think of me in New Orleans during the 1970s, what comes most to mind?
Your older sister was prettier than you and a lot more popular. But you were smarter.

I don't have an older sister. I have an older brother.
Whatever. Anyway, your father took your family on a trip to a resort. You were his favorite. He always called you Baby.

Really?
Oh yes. The waiters at the resort were all these good-looking college guys. But you fell in love with the dance instructor, even though your father hated him because he thought he got some girl pregnant. But your father ended up liking him when he saw the two of you dance at the big show at the resort.

That's not my life. That's the movie Dirty Dancing.
No, I'm pretty sure it's your life.

Really?
No. But it was a good movie.

9

Do you even know me?
Not in so many words. But I'm a big fan. Do you know how I can meet Patrick Swayze?

No. Thanks for meeting with me. You were no help at all.
You're welcome.

The last person I spoke to was Dr. Max Fenetre. He wouldn't say how I knew him but assured me he could supply a missing piece of the jigsaw puzzle that is my life. We spoke at his Beverly Hills office once he was assured that I had health insurance.

So, what would you like to tell me about myself?
I'll tell you, but only if I can be the person in italics.

No. The person who asks the questions is in italics. That's how it's done.
But I'm a doctor and therefore have much more authority than you. Ergo, I should be in italics.

I did all the other interviews in italics. I'm not going to change now.
HOW ABOUT IF I'M IN BOLD AND ALL CAPITALS, LIKE THIS?

No, it would be too distracting.
That's it, interview's over. Get out of my office, you italics hog.

YEAH, WELL GOOD-BYE TO YOU, TOO. HA, HA, HA.

Hey! I just remembered my first memory. I'm eating eggs and toast and feeling a little bit grumpy. Then I take a sip of strong black coffee and read my horoscope in the newspaper. Wait a minute. That was just an hour ago at breakfast. I guess it's possible that that's my first memory. Perhaps my philosophy is "Don't hold on to things, it will only bring you pain." Or that might not be my philosophy. I just don't remember.

a letter to my friend

or ....

*a frog in a sombrero does not a
party make*

I didn't know it was a
party for your grandmother's
90th birthday.

In digging through my old photos and letters for this book, I've discovered correspondence that brings back wonderful old memories. And, well, some not-so-wonderful memories.

Dear Morgana,

I just wanted to drop you a quick note to thank you for inviting me to your party last week. I'm not very good at parties. But I guess you know that by now. I feel awkward at them and tend to overcompensate by acting in a way that others who don't know me well might consider a tad weird. However, you know me well and besides, you're a very perceptive and, I might add, very *forgiving* person.

I guess what I'm trying to say is I'm really really really sorry for what happened. Maybe it was good, though. Maybe this will be one of those things that a little while from now you'll look back on and laugh at. Okay, maybe it will be longer than a little while. Eventually, though, after at most a few decades, there's bound to be some laughter. Isn't there? Oh God, I'm so sorry.

I know that we're good enough friends that I could just call you on the phone, but I thought a letter would be preferable for two reasons. One, often it's easier to say things in a letter than it is to say them in person. And two, you don't seem to be answering my phone calls anymore.

Sometimes nobody answers the phone—even if I let it ring over five hundred times (I've counted). At other times, somebody who sounds like you (but I'm sure isn't) answers and asks who it is. When I say "Ellen," that person (who, as I said before, I'm sure isn't you, because you are much too compassionate) immediately develops an obviously fake Russian accent and says, "She not home. She move far away to place with no phone. I begging you, please leave alone."

All that being said, let me begin my apology.

I think a lot of what happened can be traced back to the rum cake I brought over. I just looked over the recipe, and I see now that it called for two tablespoons of rum. For some reason, maybe because I was nervous because I don't cook that much, I misread that as two *bottles* of rum. It's an honest mistake, and your little nephews were eventually going to find out what a hangover is anyway.

I had at least two slices of the rum cake, and I believe that's why I blurted out that your real name is Marge. I thought everybody already knew. I also thought that everybody would find your old nickname, "Large Marge," funny. I understand now that it isn't funny. Anyway, it shouldn't bother you because you're not heavy anymore. Oh yes, I'm also sorry that I told people about your liposuction. But at least I didn't tell anybody about your breast enlargement surgery. Oh, that's right, I did. Sorry.

As for what I call "the Charades incident," for some reason I get a little competitive (okay, way too competitive) playing party games—once again, to make up for my own insecurities. That's why when Reverend Green couldn't figure out I was doing *Fried Green Tomatoes* and kept on guessing *Two Mules for Sister Sarah* (which, you have to admit, isn't even close—it doesn't even have the same number of words!) I got mad.

That in no way excuses my calling him a God damned rat @+%^#$%, *%$@-eating moron. Isn't it cute when you write curses out that way? It's too bad I didn't say it like that. Also, when I jokingly implied that he was a child molester, I had no idea about the recent trial (though I am happy to hear that all the charges have been dropped).

Now, the gift. I was under the mistaken impression (boy, hindsight is always twenty-twenty, isn't it?) that the party was for your wedding shower. That's why I got what I considered to be a gag gift. I didn't know it was a party for your grandmother's 90th birthday. Otherwise, I never would have gotten her the crotchless underwear and the coupon for a free nipple piercing.

I admit I laughed pretty hard when your grammy opened the present (sorry about the wine coming out of my nose onto your new rug—club soda should get out that stain, not cola like I tried), but I thought she was laughing, too. Now I know she was hyperventilating. I swear I've never seen anybody's face turn that red before. That is why I shouted out, "Look at her, heh heh. She looks like a big tomato!"

Not funny.

I am glad to hear that your grammy is out of the hospital. I'm the one who sent the big basket of muffins. Nobody told me she was diabetic. She only ate a few of them, and when I called the hospital they said that at most that added three days to her stay there—maybe four.

This part is the hardest to explain. I know that when you opened the door to your bedroom it looked like I was shaving your dog. Well, I was shaving your dog . . . but not for the reason you might think. I didn't say, "Hmmm, I think Marge's dog—I'm sorry, *Morgana's* dog—would look better with less hair." Though, you have to admit, the cut does give Colonel Chompers an interesting look and makes him seem quite distinguished (I don't care what the judges at the dog show say).

What happened was, in trying to spit my gum across your kitchen and into the trash can (a trick I do remarkably well, usually) I missed, and the gum landed in Colonel Chompers' fur. I tried to pull it out, but it just made matters worse. So I snuck him into your bedroom with the hope of finding some scissors and cutting the gum out. I didn't locate scissors, but I did find your Lady Gillette and thought, hey, this might work —which eventually it did. The gum came out. I am sorry that some got on your drapes. I thought they were tissue paper.

17

But, you have every right to ask, why was I wearing your bathing suit while shaving your dog? Good question. In looking for the scissors, I found the bathing suit in the third drawer of your bureau (I didn't look in your second drawer, so you have no reason to be embarrassed). I had seen that suit in a store that day and thought it might look good on me. So, I figured this was a good opportunity to try it on.

I believe you see now that there was a logical explanation for everything that happened at your otherwise very successful party.

I hope that you find it in your heart to forgive me, and we can be as good friends as we were before last weekend.

Love,
Ellen

P.S. Oh yes, I almost forgot. I'm also sorry that I bit your fiancé, I mean ex-fiancé, on the ass. Oops.

daily
affirmations

or ....

a cup of pudding a day is the
way to stay o.k.

I will wake up.

I will brush my teeth.

A POEM

Death, disease, famine
homelessness, abuse
I can't even watch
the 5 o'clock news
When did we lose control
and how do we rebel
Take a look around
we're on a rocket ship to hell
There could be an answer
it may not be too late
but it involves a transfer
try love instead of hate
All you can do
is be good to people
and hope that those people
will be good to you too
but good luck
I doubt it

When your life gets to be overwhelming, when you feel like too much of the world is depressing, there are two things you can do: One, sit in your house and feel the doom and gloom and continue to watch the news, shaking your head in resignation and saying to yourself, "Oh no, my life sucks. The world is ending, there's nothing I can do." This is one way to go. I, personally, wouldn't recommend it.

"Well," you say, "what's the *other* option?"

Here it is: If you must watch the news, turn the sound off and imagine the news anchor people are telling you all about your day. Make up happy events, adding your name into the report every third or fourth sentence.

Sing loud with wild abandonment as you get dressed in the morning (any cheery song will do).

And most important, get yourself some daily affirmations.

I do daily affirmations every day—hence the word "daily." I guess, if you're lazy, you can do weekly affirmations or monthly affirmations or even yearly affirmations. Actually, I suppose New Year's resolutions are yearly affirmations. But if you're making the same New Year's resolution every year (e.g., "I will be more popular"), and it's still not happening (e.g., "Nobody ever calls me. I'm all alone. Boo hoo."), it may be time to change your strategy. Your next yearly affirmation should be to do daily affirmations.

Daily affirmations are an important way to pick yourself up. We all have bad days and you can't always count on other people to make things better. For instance, you might say to someone, "I'm a bad person," expecting them to say in return, "Oh, no, you're not, you're one of the kindest, most thoughtful people I know." But nine times out of ten, they'll say instead, "Really. Hmmm. Hey, could you pass the Chee-tos?" And sometimes you're not even eating Chee-tos, you're eating barbecue potato chips or some weird flavored popcorn!

So, because you can't rely on other people, for your own ego you need daily affirmations. Some obvious affirmations are: "I am a good person" or "I love myself" or "I matter." But I think it's a good idea to start small. You should say things that make you feel good because they are easy to accomplish. ("I will wake up." "I will brush my teeth.") Don't push yourself. Those can be very good morning affirmations. I guess, though, if you're really depressed, and it's 8 o'clock at night, "I will wake up" would technically be an evening affirmation.

The more depressed you are, the simpler the affirmation should be. Under the right circumstances, "Who cares if I'm drunk?" is a perfectly reasonable affirmation.

Sometimes the only way you can make yourself feel better is by putting other people down. And that's okay. There is nothing wrong with that—whatever gets you through. "I'm not as fat as she is." "I have more teeth than he has." "Thank God I'm not as bone ugly as they are." These are all fine affirmations. However, it's best that when you're in public you say this kind 23 of affirmation to yourself. It can save you embarrassment and a black eye. These are silent affirmations.

You probably do affirmations without even knowing it. Every time you drive over the speed limit, you're saying, "No copper is gonna catch me speeding." And when you put that ski mask over your head, you're saying, "Nobody is going to recognize me while I rob this gas station." You're pumping yourself up and telling yourself you can succeed.

Here are some affirmations that have helped me. Use them if you'd like. They're yours free (except for what you paid for the book; if you borrowed this book from a friend or the library and you feel you should send me a few bucks, that's fine, too).

I am the world's tallest midget.

I'm a little teapot, short and stout. Here is my handle, here is my spout.

I bet nobody knows I'm crazy.

I look good in bell bottoms.

Archie would rather date me than either Betty or Veronica.

I can walk through walls. Ouch! No, I can't.

I mean for my hair to look like this.

The Great Spirit smiles on me. On me and only me. The Great Spirit hates everybody else. We're best friends.

I don't need to exercise. I have the perfect shape.

I'm smarter than my dogs. Well, smarter than one of my dogs.

I look good with back hair.

Being grubby equals being cool.

I sing better than Bonnie Raitt. I have as many Grammys as Bonnie Raitt. I am Bonnie Raitt.

It's not important to know what everybody else seems to know. I don't care how much they laugh at me.

La la la la la la la la la la la la—Talk all you want, I can't hear you—la la la la la la la la. La la la.

If I put my mind to it, I could do anything. I just don't feel like putting my mind to something. So there.

I have X-ray vision. Wait a minute. I don't. These glasses are a rip off.

I meant to get ripped off.

I've fallen and I can get up.

I'm good at watching TV.

I can come up with better affirmations than these.

ellen degeneres: road warrior

or ....

sometimes you need a map,
sometimes you need a globe,
sometimes you need a map and a
globe—but not very often

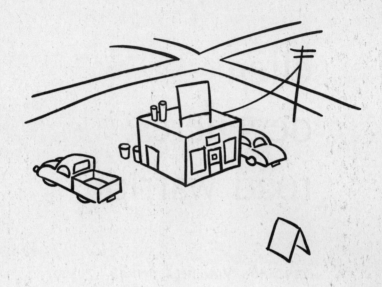

It was the mid-80's
when it wasn't considered "cool"
to know where you were.

"Aunt Ellen, tell us a story." It's so cute when the kids from the neighborhood drop on by.

They just love to hear me spin a tale. It's either that or they love that I buy liquor for them no matter how young they are. You've got to learn to drink sometime, so it might as well be with someone you can trust.

"Please, Aunt Ellen, please tell us a story," Little Tori pleaded between sips of her Margarita. Then suddenly, "Ahhh-hhh! My head hurts."

"You've just got an ice-cream headache, Dear," I assured her. Then I told her that it would go away if she pressed her tongue to the roof of her mouth and held it there for a little bit. (This really works.) Within seconds her headache was gone. "I feel so much better. You know so much, Aunt Ellen."

"Well, I've been drinking for a whole lot longer than any of you," I quipped.

We all laughed at that. After we stopped laughing and I freshened everyone's drink, I said, "So, you want to hear a story, eh?"

"Yes, yes we do, we surely, surely do! Oh yes, indeedy, doddy, duddy, we do, Aunt Ellen," Tori, Tony, Toni, Tone, Toby, Terry, and Pedro said in unison. "We want to hear a scary story."

"How about if I tell you how I broke into show business? I originally wanted to be a singer. I used to perform with the Judds. In those days we were known as Two Judds & A DeGeneres. And, well, I was always known as the funny one." I laughed.

"That's not a story!" the children cried. "We want a scary story, Aunt Ellen, not some old joke from your stand-up."

Kids are so cute. I have no idea where they get their ideas. I never did that joke in my stand-up. I may have mentioned it on

Leno or *Regis and Kathie Lee*, but I'm pretty sure I didn't do it in my stand-up. Well, not more than once or twice.

"I'll tell you the scariest story I know. It's about bad gigs that I've had." Gigs, for those of you who don't know, is plural for gig. I lit a cigarette and started my story.

"There have been many, many bad places that I have played. One of the worst was a long, narrow, dingy restaurant that may have had fifteen tables (or, if you only counted tables that didn't wobble . . . no tables). There was no way that it was created for any type of art form, whether music or comedy or anything. It was barely created for the consumption of food. I don't remember what town this was in. It could have been any town. Though, on second thought, I don't think there is a place called Anytown. I'm pretty sure it was either in the Mid West, the South, or on the East or West Coast. Or it could have been in Canada. I was traveling. I was on the road. It was the mid-eighties, when it wasn't considered 'cool' to know where you were.

"I was with some comedian, and I didn't know who he was either, even though we were doing fifteen dates together, driving from city to city. When we got to the restaurant, there was a chalkboard sitting on the street out front. It said: Soup of the Day—Cream of Asparagus. Ellen DeGeneres.

"That's when I had the Funniest Person in America title. That's the only reason I got top billing over the comedian I was with, who was the opener. He didn't even get on the chalkboard. And soup of the day had top billing over me. People would really have to want cream of asparagus soup—that would lure them in. And while they were there for the soup, well, I was just there. Nobody knew who I was. And, I'm sure my name was misspelled. My name was never spelled right. And even if it was spelled right, what did that mean to anybody? That's pretty scary right there, isn't it?"

The kids stared at me, which I took to mean, "Yes, that is pretty scary." Just then, who should come in the door but little five-year-old Mercedes and her twin brother, Oldsmobile. I had forgotten that I gave them the keys to my car to drive down to the neighborhood mart for some salted nuts and a two-pound bag of swizzle sticks. My grandmother used to say, "What's a **29** party without swizzle sticks?" And, even though I still have no idea what she was talking about, I'm never without them.

As we were passing out the nuts and the sticks, little Toby, remembering that I was in the middle of a story, asked without a hint of sarcasm, "Aunt Ellen, how did you get to be the funniest person in America?"

"This is how I got the title 'The Funniest Person in America,' " I continued, leaning back in my BarcaLounger, remembering it as if it were either yesterday or over ten years ago. "I performed stand-up comedy in New Orleans for about a year, and then the club I worked at closed down. This was through no fault of my own, but since then my philosophy has been it's just as easy to be funny without a flamethrower as it is to be with one. After that I was working in a law firm as a court runner. I worked there for about a year (until I was so out of breath I had to quit) and then I entered the Funniest Person in New Orleans contest.

"The contest was at a club before a panel of judges, and about fifteen other people competed, a lot of whom had never even been on stage before. I had a 102° fever—I was really, really sick. I almost went home, but I decided to stay. I was the last person on stage, and I won.

"They taped the show that night, and my tape was sent to the contest for the whole state of Louisiana. I won and became the Funniest Person in Louisiana. I don't even think anyone else entered (maybe Al Hirt or Archie Manning). Then my tape was sent to New York—it was put up in a fine hotel and given one hundred dollars a day spending money, which is a lot for a tape —to compete against the tapes from the other forty-nine states. Well, to make a long story short . . ."

"It's a little late for that," one of the children murmured. I couldn't tell who it was since all of them are trained ventriloquists. I decided to continue.

"So, my tape, representing Louisiana, made it to the top five from all the states. Then all five tapes went to Pee Wee Herman, Harvey Korman, and Soupy Sales—those were the judges —two of whom, if I'm not mistaken, are now on the Supreme Court. And they all picked me as the winner. So I won Funniest Person in America for Showtime based on that one 102° fever performance.

"After I won, I started traveling with that title. Showtime started taking me around to find the next year's winner. I played parking lots, supermarkets, and other places looking for next year's winner (most funny people will eventually wind up in parking lots or supermarkets). I traveled in a van with a big nose and funny glasses (on the van, not me). They wanted to make sure I didn't have too much dignity. I was on the road all the time.

"Having that title and being on Showtime got me a lot of attention. And at that time there wasn't comedy everywhere and there weren't that many comedians, so to be on television was sort of a big thing. Club owners could say, 'As seen on Showtime,' 'As seen on TV.'

"I moved to San Francisco, and suddenly I was getting jobs middling and headlining with the title The Funniest Person in America. Comedians who had been working a long time and had a lot more material and a lot more stage time and just education in general in how to handle themselves in front of an audience were a little bit peeved. And they were right to be: I was constantly blown away by the act who came before me.

"A title like that really sets you up. You know how people try to pick fights with The Heavyweight Champion of the World? People try to pick fights with The Funniest Person in America, too. And they're usually a lot easier to beat up.

"My Uncle Punch would use the title sarcastically. 'Well, if it isn't The Funniest Person in America sitting with us for Thanksgiving.'

"Or, 'Well lookie here, it's The Funniest Person in America visiting me in the hospital. I guess you wanna apologize for hitting me in the head with that turkey drumstick.'

"I don't think they have the contest anymore. They stopped after a couple of years. Where are the other people who won? I don't know. Maybe some of them are in Congress. Who knows?"

"Aunt Ellen," Tony asked as he scratched the cobra tattoo I had gotten for him that day at a cute little parlor frequented by longshoremen, "was it like winning the Miss America contest?"

"It wasn't like Miss America." I laughed. "There were no tough questions like 'How would you use your title as The Funniest Person in America to help world peace?' And the talent portion of the show was . . . being funny. Clearly that was my talent as The Funniest Person in America. There was no bathing-suit portion, funny or otherwise, and I very rarely wore the crown, except when I was at home. Sometimes, I'd wear the banner and the crown, but not out. There was no song, 'There she goes, the funniest person in America.' Some people may have sung that song, but I didn't hear it. The tape from Georgia did win Miss Congeniality, but I don't think it did the comic from Georgia—a very nice man—any good."

I realized then that I had gotten away from the scary part of my story. To quiet the children down, I spent about an hour teaching them to blow smoke rings from their cigarettes. Then

I turned off all the lights in my house (it took just a second, all I had to do was clap loud twice), held a flashlight under my chin, and said, "Now that you have some background, here are some really scary stories of bad gigs.

"One bad place I played was a marine base in front of three hundred marines. It was all men. I walked on stage and they were all screaming. They wanted me to take my clothes off, basically. They were naming parts of my body they wanted to see (some parts I hadn't even heard of). They would not shut up, and I was trying to talk to them. 'Hey, how is everybody doing?' I was trying to gain control. But these marines were just screaming at me. And I stayed up there for maybe three minutes. I realized that they were never going to shut up, and I walked off stage.

"I told the guy in charge, 'I can't do this.'

"He said, 'Whoever booked you was stupid because these men are animals, and we want them to be animals. We train them to kill. We don't want them to like art. We don't want them to appreciate art.'

" 'I just want my hundred dollars. I just want to go home. But, thank you for calling what I do *art.*'

"He kept telling me how stupid it was that I was there. Naive me, I thought these guys would be happy to see a woman, happy to hear comedy. They should have booked some stripper or something. They didn't want to hear 'The Phone Call from God,' or 'Aren't People Stupid?' or 'Don't You Hate It When You Taste Something That Tastes Bad . . . and People Want You to Taste It?'

"They'd yell, 'I'd like to taste something.' They were just horrible. No matter what I said, everything was a sexual connotation. They weren't clever. There were no double entendres. They were barely able to master the single entendre.

" 'Who here is from out of town?'

" 'I've got your out of town.'

" 'What do you mean by that?'

" 'You want me to be mean?!'

" 'You don't know what you're talking about, do you?'

" 'No.'

"But you learn from these situations; you grow from them. **33** You learn that no matter how good you are, there are certain places you walk into and there's a certain energy in that room that you cannot change. It's like having Guns 'N Roses open for Perry Como. There's no way that the audience is going to say, 'Well, this is sort of good.'

"Like in Vegas, I would open for the Pointer Sisters or Dolly Parton or Smokey Robinson. And the audience would just be waiting for them. So, while I was on, people would be eating or talking or turned around or just still being seated right in front of me. And I'd be on stage trying to do my act.

"The worst gig was the first time I played a casino. It was in Atlantic City. I opened for Lola Falana. Most of the people in the audience were between seventy and eighty. I walked out, and, needless to say, my stuff was not going over at all. I was supposed to do twenty minutes. There were no laughs and I was going faster and faster, trying to fill in the dead air. I did about ten minutes, then I walked off stage. The union guys were screaming at me, 'We have this timed so that the curtain goes up when Lola comes out. You've got to go back out there.'

" 'I can't get back out there. There's nothing else for me to say. That was the safest stuff, the easiest stuff I have.' It was a huge fight and I almost got fired. But the next day, over a pot of tea and some scones, the union guys convinced me to come back and find a way to do twenty minutes.

"So that night I had to talk slower and stall. I used this whole analogy of how, when you order the barbecued chicken entrée at a restaurant, you're choosing it because you really want the barbecued chicken. But the waitress tells you, 'Well, you know, cole slaw comes with that barbecued chicken.' And you say, 'Well, I'm not interested in the cole slaw. I just want the barbecued chicken.'

"I told the second-night audience, 'This is sort of what I am. I'm the cole slaw. Maybe you didn't really want the cole slaw, but I come with the barbecued chicken. Lola Falana is the barbecued chicken, I'm the cole slaw. If you taste the cole slaw, you may enjoy it. I know you don't really want it. And you can have your barbecue; it's not like you're not going to have your chicken. But just taste the cole slaw and see if you enjoy it. And even if you don't enjoy it, it's on the plate. It's gotta be there.'

"And that would take up a little bit of time; nobody would laugh, but it would take up time. People would sometimes yell out, 'Is it the type of cole slaw with mayonnaise or the vinegar kind? Because I'm allergic to mayonnaise.'

" 'Well then maybe you're allergic to me, ma'am. Or, maybe I don't have to be cole slaw. I could be baked beans. What wouldn't you mind so much?'

" 'I don't know. Hon,' she says, turning to her husband, 'when we're at the Kentucky Fried Chicken, what do we usually get with the chicken?'

" 'Cole slaw.'

" 'No, I'm allergic to cole slaw!'

" 'Beans?'

"Everybody broke into conversations.

" 'I don't like cole slaw.'

" 'Well, she's not saying she's cole slaw, she's saying she's something else made out of cabbage. Like, for instance . . . cole slaw.'

"And I'm going, 'Now wait a minute. Everybody listen to me. I'm just making an analogy. I'm not really cole slaw.'

"And the audience went, 'Ohhhhh,' then after a beat, 'We want Lola! We want Lola!'

"It's really scary when you have a whole room full of people seventy years old chanting, 'We want Lola.' Oh yes, I can't think of anything scarier. So, my little friends," I addressed the moon-eyed children looking up at me, "was that a scary story or what?"

The children looked at each other, then they started to chant, "We want Lola! We want Lola! We want Lola!"

And they wouldn't be quiet until I called Lola Falana and had her come over and entertain us.

But that's a story for another day.

the plane
truth

or ....

dem ain't goobers, dem's peanuts!

I never thought 3/4 of an inch
could mean so much.

I know that experts say you're more likely to get hurt crossing the street than you are flying (these, of course, would be the street-crossing experts), but that doesn't make me feel any less frightened of flying. If anything, it makes me more afraid of crossing the street. As soon as the light turns green, I run across the street as fast as I can, screaming like a madwoman. I arrive on the other side out of breath, wheezing, and clutching my stomach (or if I'm in a whimsical mood, the stomach of the person standing next to me).

So, to conquer my fear of flying, I decided to write down my feelings on a recent trip. I kept an in-flight journal (which is like an in-flight movie—but without anyone standing up in front of you so you miss the good parts, and with better sound).

I felt edgy the moment I stepped into the aircraft. That could be why I snapped at the woman in front of me. In my defense, she did ask the flight attendant a pretty stupid question: "Excuse me, where is seat 27-B?" I mean, really. But I see now that I overreacted when I screamed at her, "Well, moron, you walk in the only direction you can, and it's the 27th row, seat B—next to seat A. All righty?!" That sort of response is probably one of the many reasons why I'm not a flight attendant.

It was only when the woman (27-B) turned around to look at me that I saw she was a nun. I guess that sort of hatlike thing she wore on her head should have given me a clue, but sometimes I don't have that good an eye for details.

I tried to apologize by smiling and giving her a playful punch on the arm to let her know I was joking. Well, either my playful punch carried more of a wallop than I intended (due to the tension I feel about flying), or her advanced years made her frailer than she appeared, or she was just a big old ham (which is my theory), but the nun shouted out, "Owww!" and rubbed her arm like she was in pain. She rolled up her sleeve and . . .

you know, that bruise could *easily* have been there before I hit her.

My good friend Jasmine (at least I think that's her name; I'm so scared that it's affecting my already rattled memory; I know that it's the name of a tea, so if it's not Jasmine, it's either Earl Grey or Hibiscus) told me that a good way to combat fear is to chant. So all the way to my seat I was chanting, "I'm going to die, I'm going to die, oh sweet Lord, I'm going to die." It didn't work. If anything, I was more petrified when I got to my seat (27-A). Even seeing the familiar face of the nun in 27-B (who seemed to flinch when she saw me) didn't calm me down.

So here I am, sitting in my seat, working on my journal. Hey, there's a fly on this plane. I am so scared of flying, I can't imagine how flies do it all day, every day. But, then again, that's what a fly does, fly. It's his job. What's going through that fly's mind? He's looking out the window and probably saying to himself, "Wow, look how high up I am. I've never gotten up this high, I am going very, very fast, and I'm not really working any harder than I usually do."

This fly just happened to wander onto a plane in Los Angeles. Several hours later it is going to get off in New York City. I'm concerned it will be disoriented, and not just from jet lag and being improperly dressed for New York, but more in a *Home Alone* 2 kind of way.

A bunch of flies will probably be waiting as it gets off the plane. They'll all be hugging, blocking the way. Nobody will get by. There will even be a chauffeur holding a tiny sign that says FLY. I'll be relieved to see he has friends there. Well, I'm assuming it's a *he*. It's so hard to tell unless you hold them really still and look closely, and I don't want to do that on the plane with people around. That's something you should do at home —alone.

Aghhhhhh! What was that? "Fuck, we're going to crash!!!"

Oh, I wish I hadn't shouted that out loud. It was just the beverage cart rumbling by. Being on a plane just freaks me out. Any little movement, and suddenly it's like I have Tourette's syndrome. Anything at all—"Fuck! Shit!" I don't even curse. I never curse. It's so embarrassing. "Pardon me, Sister, I am sorry, I . . . I was frightened. Pray for me."

Now she's going to turn on that little air thing above her. Maybe I'm paranoid, but I think it takes power away from the plane somehow. I get mad if people next to me use theirs.

"Sister, don't use that, that's . . . Dang! Shut if off! I'll hit ya! Shut if off!!"

The nun just left to find a different seat. Some people are so touchy. I'm sure she didn't learn that little hand gesture in her convent, either.

As scary as this flight is, it's nothing compared to those tiny Buddy Holly planes that I've had to fly in to get to different stand-up performances. Oh God, those little propeller planes, those little eight-seater tiny planes where you can actually see the pilots in the cockpit. They're reading through some manuals like *So You Want to Be a Pilot*. They're just flipping through the pamphlet trying to figure out which buttons to push to land the plane.

I've got to relax somehow. Why didn't I think of this sooner? I'll recline my seat. Oh, that makes all the difference. That ¾ of an inch between upright and reclined is the difference between agony and ecstasy. I never thought ¾ of an inch could mean so much. *Now* I can sleep. When I get home, I'm going to put some gizmo in my chairs so that they go back ¾ of an inch, too. I wouldn't overdo it like the guy sitting in front of me. His seat goes so far back that his head is practically in my lap. I can pretty much read his newspaper.

I'd better not get too comfortable in my ¾ of an inch recline because toward the end of the flight, the flight attendant is going to say, "You're going to have to put your seat in the upright position for landing." They're so adamant about that every single time, like that's gonna make a difference. Because if we crash, the investigators are going to say, "Oh, that's a shame, her seat was reclined ¾ of an inch. When will they learn? What was that—thirty thousand feet? She could have made that. Sheesh. If only she'd been upright."

Being reclined isn't working. I'm still freaking out. I know what I need. "Oh, flight attendant. Oh, ma'am." You have to talk nice to the flight attendants because they're all arrogant little bitches. Unless, of course, you happen to be a flight attendant or are related to or are friends with one—then you are the absolutely lovely exceptions to this rule. But the rest of them, they have this attitude. And they can afford to have the attitude, because they have the power—they have the peanuts.

They have these six peanuts that we need. Six peanuts. Somebody could offer that to you on the street, and you'd say, "I don't want that shit—get that away from me. Six peanuts? No-oh." Somehow they've done research. They know that the higher we go, the more we need nuts. And we go crazy if we don't get them.

"Miss, I didn't get my, uh—my peanuts. And I'd really appreciate it if you gave me some. They're good, aren't they? I've never been able to get them on the ground either. At least not ones this good. Thank you. Oh, thank you."

Fuck, what was that! "We're going to crash!" Oops, false alarm. It's just the food cart coming down the aisle.

I think they only give you six peanuts so that you don't spoil your appetite for the disgusting meal that's soon to follow. You never hear anybody say, "You know, I can't finish that. Could you wrap that up for me please? That was delicious. It's just too much. I'm stuffed! What was that, pigeon?"

But we do get excited about it, don't we? "Oh, here comes the cart, put down the tray! La la la la. Put down your tray! They're starting on the other side first. Hurry! Hurry! Those people over there—they're eating. Those people are eating."

This is the tiniest food I've ever seen in my entire life. I 43 guess they figure everything's relative. You get that high up, you look out the window, "Well, it's as big as that house down there. I can't eat all that. Look at the size of that. It's as big as a house. Me thinking I could eat all that! Ha! Split that steak with me. Now *that's* a steak." Any kind of meat that you get— chicken, steak, anything—has grill marks on each side, like somehow we'll actually believe there's an open-flame grill in the front of the plane.

Salads are always two pieces of dead lettuce and salad dressing that comes in that astronaut package. As soon as you open it, it's on your neighbor's lap. "Could I just dip my lettuce, ma'am? Hm, that's a lovely skirt. What is that, silk?" But you know, should that happen, club soda's gonna get that stain out immediately.

That's the answer to anything you ask up there, I don't know if you've noticed that.

"Excuse me, I have an upset stomach."
"Club soda, be right back."
"Excuse me, I spilled something."
"Club soda, be right back."
"Ooh, the wing is on fire!"
"Club soda, be right back."

I thought the food would make me feel less frightened. But it didn't. Maybe if I stretch my legs and go to the restroom it will help.

That was the tiniest bathroom I've ever been in. I guess they figure since the food is so tiny, the bathrooms should be minuscule, too. I read a book once where two people had sex in an airplane bathroom. I don't see how that's possible. I barely had enough room to sit down. There is a lit sign in there that reads: "Return to Seat." "Return to Cabin." Why do they think that needs to be lit? Because we'll relax in there for a little while? "Miss, bring my peanuts in here, please. This is *beautiful*. The water is so blue, it reminds me of the Mediterranean. I don't ever want to leave."

You have no concept of time when you're in there—it's like a casino: no windows, no clocks. I could be the only one to get up out of my seat to go to the bathroom—everybody else is sound asleep when I go—but after I've been in there for what I think is thirty seconds, I open the door and everyone in the plane is lined up, looking at their watches, making me feel like I've been in there forever.

And now I've got to explain the smell that was in there before I went in there. Does that ever happen to you? It's not your fault. You've held your breath, you just wanna get out, and now you open the door and you have to explain, "Oh! Listen, there's an odor in there and I didn't do it. It's bad. You might want to sprinkle some club soda, if you uh . . ."

I think my only hope of escaping my mind-numbing fear is to sleep; to sleep and perchance to dream. The only trouble is when I fall asleep on a plane, I always have a nightmare. . . .

I'm in a department store walking through the area with the makeup counters—then all of a sudden I'm a penguin on ice skates—Florence Henderson is cooking macaroni and cheese in my kitchen and my brother has gained 200 pounds and is being fed by three Haitian women wearing disco clothes and in the background the Bee Gees are arguing over what outfits to wear for their big comeback.

Then I turn into myself again and Bruce Willis calls me up and asks me to go out with him and drink some wine coolers. So, we're sitting in an outdoor cafe in Italy called Louis'. He's telling me his life was meaningless until I came into it. I tell him I'm not ready to make a commitment. Just then I give birth to three sets of twins: they're nine years old, one has false teeth, two are great dancers. The rest move to South Dakota for schooling.

45

Now I'm dancing with Lewis and Clark (my two children) and an iguana who's making eyes at me (he's not that good of a dancer). Bruce punches him in the nose. The iguana turns into Sean Penn, who knocks Bruce unconscious. Sean and I start walking, and he tells me his life has been meaningless up until he met me, then we see one of those photo booths, four for a dollar. He urges me to pose with him. So we get in and have our pictures taken. He covers his face for all of them. He asks me to keep them. He beats up the machine.

I fly back to the States alone. The pilot announces, "Ladies and Gentlemen, we'll be landing in ten minutes. Ellen, I just want to say my life has been meaningless until you came into it." We land. I go to the baggage claim, and my bag comes out first. I think to myself, "Ellen, you must be dreaming—that's impossible. . . ."

"Fuck, we're going to crash!!"

False alarm. The plane just landed. I guess I'm alive. Oh well, that wasn't so bad. But what about that dream! I don't know what it means. I'm pretty sure it's sexual.

Maybe it just means I shouldn't be flying.

ellen's new hobby

You can do it, Ellen.
Get out of the house, find your
path and follow your heart.

I need a hobby. Something to pass my time—a goal I can work toward. I've tried knitting, square dancing, social work. I need to have passion about something. Here I am, sitting at my kitchen table, staring at my pancakes and coffee, feeling the emptiness of a life with no meaning.

It's like I'm sitting in a car but the engine is idling. I'm not even on the road—just off to the side. I see the others swoosh by me. I can recognize the shapes of the cars but not the direction they're going. I'm alone, all alone in a car on the side of the road.

My dogs are staring at me, trying to give me hope. "You can do it, Ellen," they say. "Get out of the house, find your path and follow your heart." I want to find it so bad, I do. But all I can do is turn on my TV and watch *Regis and Kathie Lee*. I can answer those trivia questions. Maybe they'll call me and put a pin in my city. I want a pin; I want to share a hot-air popcorn popper with number 35. That's who I would pick.

I just saw a flash of a woman with dogs on the screen. She races or something; she used the word *Iditarod*. I looked it up in the dictionary, but it wasn't there. I was so upset, I started to cry and scream, "Why—why—why?" I was pounding on the table with my closed fists. I was filled with anger—raging with fury— I was a wild stallion rearing up on its hind legs, snorting and whinnying and kicking and . . . Wait a minute. Hold on just a cotton-pickin' minute. This is passion I'm feeling. This word *Iditarod* has moved me. I must find out what this *Iditarod* is and do it—I will *Iditarod* and I will win.

JOURNAL ENTRY

I am beginning to feel frustrated. It is my fourth week of training for the Iditarod and I am seeing very little progress, if any at all. The big race is two months away, and I worry I won't be ready. I already have one strike against me: My sled barely moves along the concrete-paved roads.

Having only two dogs is also not helping. Since I don't believe in hitting, I certainly won't strike my dogs just to make them pull me. So I encourage them strongly. "Please, let's go, come on." But they come toward me and get in the sled. Seems they're conditioned to come *to* me when I speak, not away. I've tried dog biscuits, but as I place them down several yards ahead of the dogs, by the time I run back to get in the sled, they've run to get the biscuits without me in it. Also, one of my dogs is rather small so the times we do move at all, it's in circles—the larger one sets our course off balance.

I am sweating so much in those big Eskimo clothes because of the warm California climate. I should warn others to wear a cooler version here. Ah, well, I must not give up. It's a dream. I will race! I can't let the neighborhood children's silly taunts stop me. Let them laugh all they want. I will race in the Iditarod one day.

JOURNAL ENTRY

I've given up returning phone calls. I've given up my so-called "normal" life. I can't be bothered. The race is but a month away. I eat, drink, and sleep Iditarod.

I've begun to question aspects of my training. I had heard that carbo loading was good, but now I am not so sure. My dogs have gotten fat and lethargic. I may need to change their diet of spaghetti, potatoes, pound cake, and ice cream. Now, when I bring them to the sled, they just roll over and fall asleep. Sometimes, to my eternal shame, I do the same.

Perhaps I should quit. No, no, no!! I cannot allow a negative thought. My will cannot be broken or bent. I must continue chanting my mantra:

51

Icanarod, Iwillarod, Iwinarod, Iditarod.

Icanarod, Iwillarod, Iwinarod, Iditarod. Icanarod, Iwillarod, Iwinarod, Iditarod. If I chant loudly enough, I can barely hear the jeering from the neighborhood children. They are ignorant philistines. No matter how many times I correct them, they get it wrong. I scream to deaf, uncaring ears, "It's pronounced *Iditarod*, not idiot!"

I have ended my quest for corporate sponsorship. The only offer came from a place called Uncle Huey's Dry Cleaning and Donut Shop and only if I wore a vest with their motto: "If you get some jelly donut on your clothes, we'll clean it before you're finished with your second cup of coffee." I have too much pride. I will not look ridiculous, so I turned them down. They can keep their $35.

JOURNAL ENTRY

I do worry that I will not be ready in time to race the Iditarod after all. It is only two weeks away, and I have made little progress. The dogs sense when we are about to begin training. They watch me get dressed and know that when the big boots come out, we are headed for the sled. It's 87°, unusually hot for this time of year. I have lost fifteen pounds just from wearing these big bundly clothes and sitting in my sled, but I must get used to the bulkiness.

I have made some progress, though. Last Thursday, Bootsie, Muffin, and I were out in the street sitting there, same as every morning—we've chosen to go out at 3:00 A.M. to avoid both traffic and cruel neighborhood children. Suddenly, Bootsie and Muffin took off with a start that caught me unawares (I had dozed off). I was thrown from the sled and the dogs ran for a half a mile or so. I caught up to them and encouraged them profusely. "Good doggies," I said. "Good dogs—two good girls." I'm not sure, but I think they saw a squirrel or something. It's too bad there wasn't another squirrel to get us back home. We walked; I carried the sled. I sure hope we'll be ready. Maybe there are squirrels in Alaska.

JOURNAL ENTRY

Well, we're in Alaska and I'll tell you something, it's *cold*. It's so cold it's snowing—looks like it has been for a while. The dogs are not taking to the snow the way I'd hoped they would. Muffin, the smaller one, is being downright stubborn, refusing to step foot (or paw) in the snow. I can't really blame her—she sinks into it so far, her ears are barely sticking out.

I feel we are in trouble with both dogs pulling—and there's no way to try with only Bootsie. Also, Bootsie has, it seems—and this is terrible timing—just gone into heat. I was debating whether I should neuter her before the race and then I totally forgot. You can imagine the scene she's causing. I've never seen her act this way. I keep apologizing to all of the other contestants.

So far, no one is talking to me. They're kind of snobbish folks. And real serious about this race. I think some are cheating, too. Some have as many as eight dogs. They must all know each other—all of the dogs look alike and are well-behaved. They look at my dogs a lot—probably very curious about the breed. It's hard to tell what they are with their little sweaters on.

Uh oh, I hear a ruckus outside. Sounds like Bootsie is into some trouble with other dogs. I'll sign off for now. The big day is soon upon us.

JOURNAL ENTRY

Anchorage, Alaska. Five A.M.

I haven't been sleeping well. I'm very worried about the race. It starts tomorrow, and since arriving here I've learned a lot more about this event. For instance, you're supposed to have somewhere between fourteen and twenty dogs per sled. Wow! That's crazy. I mean—where do all of these people live that they're allowed to own that many dogs? I know for my own neighborhood there is a zoning law that prohibits a person from having any more than three dogs. Nevertheless, I must adapt to the circumstances and move forward. I will go to the local animal shelter today and get more dogs. Since Bootsie and Muffin are somewhat familiar with the routine, I won't need the full twenty dogs. I'll just get fifteen. A nice seventeen will do just fine. I figure these dogs will be so grateful to be adopted they'll do anything I ask of them. After the race I'll simply find good, loving homes for them.

JOURNAL ENTRY

Uh oh. I think I'm in trouble. For some reason the shelter didn't have that many dogs. I got seven—that's all they had—and eight cats (I was desperate). I see no reason why I can't train the cats to pull. I've seen movies and TV shows where they use cats (for what exactly I don't remember). Besides, with the nine dogs total, they should be able to get it going, and once we have momentum it should be easy pulling for the cats (well, kittens —they're ten weeks old). Maybe I'll just keep the kittens in the sled with me. They can't add any weight. I wonder if I can push the sled in addition to the dogs pulling or at least just run alongside. I've picked up a pamphlet on the race—hopefully I will get a little more insight on this Iditarod.

Bye for now.

JOURNAL ENTRY

Oh my— Maybe this wasn't such a good idea. I'm afraid I'm not as prepared as I would like to be. My intentions were good, but Bootsie is having a problem with the kitties. I've tried to introduce them slowly so as to avoid the problem we had the first day. I've never seen Bootsie so aggressive. Luckily, I got there in time to stop her violent charges at the poor kitties. I can't imagine why she hates them so!

The race started yesterday. I hope I can catch up. It shouldn't be that hard. I've attached a small motor to my sled, which should help matters somewhat. I plan on leaving tonight.

Over and out.

JOURNAL ENTRY

Things have gotten worse and worse. All the other racers are two days ahead of me. I hate them. They are a distasteful group whose juvenile jeering made me yearn for the taunts of my neighborhood children. I dream of wiping the smiles off their smug, pudgy faces. How dare they call me a Sheila Disco Musher?

But I fear that my dreams of revenge will just be dreams. The motor on my sled didn't work, probably because it wasn't attached to anything. All it did was make a lot of noise, weigh down the sled, and scare the cats.

I must keep my spirits up. Not so much for myself as for my team. I must not give up hope. If we do not feel like winners, we cannot win. To that end I will head to downtown Anchorage today to get the three poodles on my team pedicures.

Whenever I ask myself, "Why go on?" I must answer, "Why not." Miracles do happen.

Icanarod, Iwillarod, Iwinarod, Iditarod.

JOURNAL ENTRY

I won! I won! They say I didn't. They say I cheated. They say I've been disqualified. All I know is I finished first. My team and I were the first ones to get from Anchorage to Nome.

They can bitch and moan as much as they please. Nowhere in the rules does it say you can't use a Winnebago. It was a stroke of genius and a bit of luck. Who would have guessed that there was an auto dealership across the street from the dog groomer? With the sled and dogs and cats in the back, we just took off down the freeway. We beat the nearest racer by two days and we rarely went over fifty-five miles an hour, mainly because Muffin gets nauseous if I drive any faster.

As for the other Iditaroders, I have never seen such a group of sore losers in my life. But I pity them more than hate them. They're just jealous.

I can't get rid of my posse (that's what I've started calling my team). To hell with neighborhood rules, I'm keeping them all. Maybe I'll return to defend my title next year. Back to back!

JOURNAL ENTRY

Life has no meaning again. I gaze into the abysmal void that is my soul and all that is reflected back is my own emptiness. I am bored and restless. The high of being the Iditarod champion did not last long. I need a new challenge. But what?

My posse, my team, my cats and dogs: They're listless as well. I try to maintain a happy exterior for their sake, but they're not fooled.

Once again I'm watching *Regis and Kathie Lee*. Even Kathie Lee's stories about Cody fail to cheer me up. Before I turn off the set and do God knows what, I see an image: a boat skating across the sea. A woman mentions the America's Cup, the world's premier yacht race. Yes!!!!

I bet there are no rules about having pets as part of your crew. Me and my posse start training tomorrow. Until I get a yacht, we'll just use an inflatable raft in my pool.

The dream lives.

ellenvision

....

Nuns were very popular
in the 60's.

I feel extremely lucky to have my own TV show. Every day I pinch myself because I'm sure I must be dreaming. Actually, I don't pinch myself. It's one of my manager's jobs to pinch me and say, "You ain't dreamin', kid!" Then I pinch him, he pinches me back, and it usually ends up in a slap fight. Sometimes the slap fight lasts until midnight. Then we call it a day, go to sleep, and repeat it all again the next morning.

I guess what I'm trying to say is that I'm so happy that my show is as good, and as based in reality, as it is. You wouldn't believe some of the shows that were offered me by network executives before I accepted *Ellen* (which, by the way, is named for Ellen Burstyn).

In one show presented to me, I was going to be a single news producer for a small TV station in Minneapolis. I said, "That sounds an awful lot like *Mary Tyler Moore*." They replied, "Who's going to remember?"

Other shows I was offered included *Hello Ellen* (with MacLean Stevenson), *Ellen the Chimp Lady*, and a sitcom version of *The Piano*—I was going to play the Holly Hunter part, and either Siegfried or Roy was going to play the Harvey Keitel role.

I think the worst idea I was subjected to was a show called *Inky Dinky Do*. "*Inky Dinky Do*," I said, "what's it about?" The network executive said, "We don't know yet. All we've come up with is the title."

I don't mean to imply that I haven't gotten weird notes from the network about my show now. They'd like me to develop some magic powers, like the ability to see through lead or bend spoons with my mind. But no matter how weird my show—*Ellen* —might get, nothing compares to how weird TV was during the sixties.

Not that there aren't bad shows on now, but at least they kind of have a base in reality. Well, okay, *Melrose Place* doesn't.

The sixties were when hallucinogenic drugs were becoming really, really big. And I don't think it's a coincidence that we had the type of shows that we had then, like *The Flying Nun*.

If you think about it, nuns were very popular in the sixties. They must have had a good publicist then. They had *The Sound of Music*, about a nun. They had *The Singing Nun*—remember her? "Dominique a nique a nique a Dominique . . ." So they figure, "Hey, the nuns are popular, let's do a TV show." But I think it was just about nuns until they got the Network Notes. "Nuns are good. People will watch. But, couldn't they fly or something? People like flying."

I'm just surprised there were no copycat shows, like *The Swimming Rabbi* or *The Leaping Episcopalian*. Because, no matter how bizarre a show is, if it's popular, someone is going to try to imitate it. *Bewitched* came on and one year later it was *I Dream of Jeannie*. "No, they're different. On one she twitches her nose, on the other she blinks. But the most important thing is, one's a witch and the other's a genie. It's so different it's not even funny."

Other similar shows were *The Addams Family* and *The Munsters*; *Gilligan's Island* and *Lost in Space*; *Mr. Ed* and *My Mother the Car* (one is a talking horse, the other a talking car—they're both transportation); *Gunsmoke* and *60 Minutes* (well, they both have a bunch of guys and one girl).

My Mother the Car has to be the weirdest show ever. It even tops *The Flying Nun*. A man's mother dies and is reincarnated as a car. It *could* happen. I mean, a talking toaster or talking can opener, an ironing board or a Ping-Pong table—*those* would be ridiculous. But a talking car? That's much more likely.

Somewhere along the way to putting this show on the air, drugs had to be involved. It was the sixties. To me it sounds like the last idea you have, and you mention it, kind of embarrassed, after all your other ideas have been rejected. "I came up with this one at 3:00 in the morning. I don't know . . . Well, it's a talking car—you know, like they have—and it's this guy's mother . . . I guess."

Now he might not have been zoned out on boo or goof-balls, but the network guy who bought it, man, *he* had to be on something. "Right, it talks. Just like a person talks. I dig it. Write it up. I'll give you more notes after I tie-dye my shirt and drive up to San Francisco to see the Grateful Dead. Wow. Look at my fingers. They're funny."

I saw Jerry Van Dyke, the star of *My Mother the Car*, in person around the time that show was on the air, but it's kind of embarrassing how I saw him. The only major trip that my family ever took was to Los Angeles, Disneyland, and Anaheim. We took a train and that was kind of fun. My parents told my brother and me that it was an airplane, but we figured out after the first thousand miles that they were lying. We went to Hollywood and saw the set where *Gilligan's Island* was shot. That was every bit as exciting as you could imagine.

While we were in Hollywood, my mom spotted Jerry Van Dyke walking down some street. It was a big deal for us to see a celebrity, so, when my mother saw him she screamed, "There's Dick Van Dyke's brother!" He looked around kind of uncomfortably. Even as a child, I was humiliated. I just knew that that wasn't a good thing.

I don't remember how old I was at the time. Maybe my parents would remember or perhaps even Jerry Van Dyke.

I guess they had another talking-car show in the eighties: *Knight Rider*. That was much different, though. It was a drama and not a comedy.

Actually, of all those odd shows, *Mr. Ed* doesn't sound so weird. I guess that's because my Uncle Cookie had a talking horse. Well, it was really a dog with a saddle on it, but my Uncle Cookie thought it was a horse. He was blind and a little loopy.

We didn't want to break his heart. It was all he had, that horse. Or dog. It was a small dog. But he never saw a horse, so he didn't know how big it was supposed to be.

Nobody heard him talk but my Uncle Cookie. The dog would be lying on the floor (actually it was dead) and my Uncle would say, "That's a good one, Spot. He's telling a joke now."

That's right, Uncle Cookie.

I went to a psychic

or ....

baloney is just salami with an inferiority complex

You have a brother or a sister
or you are an only child.

A lot of people who know I'm writing a book ask me, "So, do you think it's going to be any good? Well, do you?"

It's hard to tell how successful or good anything is going to be. And, to be honest, it makes me a little nervous. That's why I decided to do the only rational thing: go to a psychic. I mean, what's the use of putting in a lot of hard work if this book is going to be a flop? I could better use my time doing other stuff, like becoming a professional ballerina or flossing.

The first psychic I went to wasn't that good. Do you know how some people go to student beauticians to save a little money? I went to a student psychic. There was a little psychic academy in a mini-mall between a video store and a frozen-yogurt place. It was called Gus's Psychic School.

My student psychic was named Chuck. He was an ex-soldier who was going to Psychic School on the GI Bill. The first thing he said to me was "You are at a crossroads and confused. There are questions you want answered." "Well, yeah," I said, "that's why I'm here. Why else would I go to a psychic?" I should have gotten suspicious when he said, "How am I supposed to know? What am I, Kreskin?"

Chuck said "Oooooooo" and raised his hands in the air every time he made a prediction. I guess he thought it looked like he was communicating with powerful entities in the spirit world, but to me it looked like he was auditioning for a minstrel show. I knew he was bad because he wouldn't say anything without first consulting his Time/Life book on unexplained phenomena.

His predictions were kind of vague, to say the least. "I see you pouring some kind of liquid into your mouth out of a cylindrical object. This object, it's made of . . . glass. After you pour the liquid into your mouth, you will no longer be thirsty."

"There is someone important in your life whose name starts with either the letter E . . . C . . . B . . . F . . . or M through W."

"You have a brother or a sister. Either that or you are an only child." I told him I had a brother; he seemed proud of himself, then went back to psychicing.

"Your brother knows how to drive." As a matter of fact he does. He drives an ambulance. He's not a paramedic or anything, he just got a good deal on it. It doesn't get very good mileage, but the upside is he's never late to meetings.

"On Letterman tonight, Dave's guests will be Angela Lansbury and Sting." I had to tell him that wasn't a prediction, it was a blurb from *TV Guide*. He tried to cover by saying he has never read *TV Guide*, even though there was one on his desk with the crossword puzzle half done. Then he said that so much came to him, he couldn't remember if it was a prediction or if he read it somewhere.

I asked him about my past lives, hoping that I had been Cleopatra or, at the very least, someone who once had lunch with Cleopatra. He told me that once I had been a monkey, but that in my last life I was a spring roll at a Chinese restaurant. Now that's ridiculous, even though it does explain a recurring nightmare where I'm held upside down over a dish of hot mustard sauce.

At a beautician school, there is a teacher present at all times to advise the student and make sure things don't get too out of hand. At the psychic academy, the psychic teacher wasn't there. He would just call in by phone now and then from his condo in Hawaii to tell his students he knew they were doing a good job. Or he would call and say things like "Tell that woman there's something caught in her teeth."

The student psychic finally admitted that he wasn't very good. He was, however, able to predict where I would find a good psychic. The session wasn't a total waste because he gave me a dollar-off coupon for the frozen-yogurt place next door.

You could tell the woman he referred me to was good because she opened the door before I rang the bell. Then she said, "You must be Ellen." Well, that was the capper. Because Ellen is my name and all. Sure I had an appointment, and she could have been looking through the keyhole, but I prefer to think she had finely honed psychic powers.

It seems most psychics have names like Esmerelda or Cassandra—spooky kinds of names. Mine was named Shari Lewis. Not the woman with Lambchop the puppet, just somebody with the same name. I wouldn't trust a psychic who used a puppet. I don't think it's because I'm prejudiced or anything. It's just that it would disturb me to have a little puppet voice say, "You will be successful as long as you never get up on stilts. Avoid *Circus of the Stars*—don't even watch it."

The psychic knew that I was nervous about writing a book. This might be because the first thing I said to her was "I'm nervous about writing a book." She looked me in the eye (or possibly both eyes, I don't remember) and without raising her arms or saying, "Ooooooooo," she made her predictions. The good news, she said, was that my book is going to be on best-seller lists for over twenty-five years and win a ton of awards (literally a ton; they'll actually weigh them at one point). The bad news, though, was that I was going to have to sit down and actually write the book. I was kind of hoping that elves would come in the middle of the night while I was sleeping and write a best-seller for me; the psychic told me that though this wasn't impossible (she claimed one or two of Danielle Steel's books were written this way) in my case it was highly unlikely. Bummer.

Then she took out her tarot cards. She wasn't able to get a very good reading, so then she took out a deck of regular cards. An hour and a half later she had won $150 off of me playing gin rummy. So you can see, she's a very good psychic, even though what she really wants to do is deal blackjack in Vegas.

The good psychic would pick up the phone before it rang. Of course, it's possible there was nobody on the other line. Once she said, "God bless you." I said, "I didn't sneeze." She looked deep into my eyes and said, "You will, eventually." And, damn if she wasn't right. Two days later I sneezed. It felt eerie. Not the sneeze, just that she predicted it.

It sounds like a real L.A. thing to do, going to a psychic. I was thinking this as I drove away from her home in my Mercedes convertible on my way to pick up my dog from his personal trainer. What's great about this trainer is that she also does my dog's colors. It turns out my dog is an Autumn, which explains why he looks so good in an olive green sweater.

Well, as I was driving, the phone rang. This was weird in itself, because the psychic had predicted that I would get a phone call later in the day. As it turned out, it was my psychic calling. While we were chatting, I got a fax reminding me to call my bird psychiatrist.

Now a bird psychiatrist isn't an actual bird; that would be ridiculous. He's a human psychiatrist that deals with my bird's problems. You just call him up on the phone, tell him what's bothering your bird, and he tells you how to deal with it. He's a bit cheaper than an actual psychiatrist—no pun intended—so sometimes I call him up with one of my problems and pretend that it's one of my bird's problems. Actually, I don't even own a bird.

"Well my bird is thinking about starting a new relationship. The problem is that this other bird reminds him of somebody else, somebody who had hurt him in a previous relationship.

My bird had been rejected and didn't take it well. He drank a lot of fermented seed juice and didn't go out much for a long time. And when he did, he took out his pain on other birds.

"Also, my bird, Paco, who has a sitcom that's called *Paco* (he's a very funny bird), is worried about a book he's supposed to write. So, he's not sure this is the best time to start a relationship.

"Paco had an interesting dream recently. I sensed the dream. I know him well enough to pick up the dreams, but not well enough to actually help him. That's why I called you. He had this dream that he was being held upside down and dipped into a dish of hot mustard sauce . . .

"Oh, I see, he probably was a spring roll in a past life."

I put on the answering machine, so I wouldn't get any more phone calls as I drove. I felt content. So, I guess what I'm trying to say is that I have a good feeling about this book. That's what you asked, right?

how to explain sex to a child

or ....

where there's a corn chip, there's bound to be hot sauce

Oooo baby, I feel lucky tonight.

Hey, Debbie, this is Ellen. That's a real cute phone message. You sounded just like Elmer Fudd. Geez, I hope you were trying to sound like Elmer Fudd. If you weren't, I'm terribly sorry. Thanks for saying that you'd watch my house while I'm gone next week on vacation to the Luxembourg Soft Cheese and Jazz Festival. I know you said you would water the plants, bring in the mail and turn some lights on so that it looks like somebody is home. But if it's not too much of an imposition, could you also make sure that the mobile over the crib isn't tangled? Otherwise, the baby is just going to get bored. I never knew having a kid was so much responsibility! Bye bye.

I'm just joking. I don't have a baby. I do, however, have a mobile and a crib. I enjoy those things, so I have them. And, even though I don't have a baby, I have hired a nanny. In case I decide to have a baby, it's nice to know that Bok Choy is there. (To keep him in practice, I have him read me a bedtime story every night and occasionally I let him burp me.)

I want to have a child. I really do. I think about it every day —and every day I change my mind: I want one now. I'll wait a year. I want one now. I'll wait a year. Well, you get the idea.

I think that part of my dilemma is that even though I want to have a baby, I don't want to *have* the baby. I can't imagine *having* the baby. Giving birth is just so much pain. I know it's a beautiful child you end up with. I'm aware of that. But if I want a new washer and dryer, I wouldn't necessarily want to *have* a new washer and dryer, if you know what I mean (and if you don't, I really don't care to explain it in any more detail).

I don't think I could go through that pain (having the *child* —let's just forget the washer and dryer now, okay?). A lot of women I know believe in natural childbirth. No matter how much discomfort they're in, they refuse to take drugs. Mercy, mercy me! Just thinking about that pain makes me want to take drugs (sometimes I even drive down to the hospital and demand an epidural).

I don't need a baby growing inside of me for nine months, either. For one thing, there's morning sickness. If I'm going to feel nauseous and achy when I wake up, I want to achieve that state the old-fashioned way: getting good and drunk the night before. I know that a woman glows when she's pregnant, and that sounds neat. But, I can get a pretty good glow by enjoying a steam bath followed by some assorted skin creams. The thing that I don't understand most is when a pregnant woman joyfully talks about feeling her baby kick. To me, getting kicked isn't as big a thrill as others make it out to be. I've never liked getting kicked from the outside, why should I feel any different about an inside kick?

But I would like to have a child. So, one day I'd like to adopt a baby who needs a loving home and be a mother who will adore him or her and teach it important things. I think I'd make a great mother. I'm great with kids. I know this because I'm the godmother to a precious little two- or five-year-old boy or girl (I'm not sure of the specifics). I probably would be overprotective of my child, though. She (if it's a girl) or he (if it's not a girl) would always have to wear a helmet (even if it's just to eat cereal; those spoons can be mighty dangerous!); would be on one of those protective leashes until, at least, senior year of high school; and would, in general, be raised like people raise veal—confined to a crate by itself somewhere.

I think my best quality as a mother would be the ability to communicate complex ideas simply. I think all parents dread the old "How are babies made" question. I know my parents had a problem explaining this to me.

"Mommy, Daddy—how are babies made?"
"Well, Ellen honey, there's an egg."
"Like a chicken egg?"

"No, smaller."

"Like a robin's egg?"

"No, much smaller—it's very small. And Daddy gives Mommy . . . Well, there's a Papa Bear and a Mama Bear and the Mama Bear has the baby in her tummy—"

"So I grew in a bear's stomach?"

75

"No, but if you were a bear you would've."

"But I'm not a bear?"

"No, you're a little girl."

"So, where did I grow?"

"In Mommy's tummy."

"How did I get there?"

"Daddy gave her special sauce."

"Like McDonald's?"

"Who knows? Maybe."

"How did he give it to her? In a hamburger?"

"Okay. Yes."

"I like hamburgers. Good night."

"Good night, sleep tight."

I know that I could do a much better job answering that question than my parents. Other people sense this, too. In fact, hardly a day goes by when somebody doesn't ask me, "Ellen, how can I explain sex to my children?" Unfortunately, it's always the same person who is asking me that question. He's the man who runs the cheese shop I go to—Cheeses 'N' Things it's called (I've always been afraid to ask what the 'N' Things are). Anyway, this man's only child works in the store with him, is in his mid-twenties, and from the way he handles a sharp cheddar, can probably explain more about sex to his father than vice versa.

Whatever the case, I'm sure there are many other reasonably sane people who are troubled by this problem. And the more children there are (and I'm not sure where these children are coming from), the more explaining about sex there is to be done.

By sex I mean, of course . . . sex. You know what I'm saying. There are many different types of sex, but for the purpose of this explanation I'm just talking about . . . you know, sex. In other words, you might have two consenting adults, a coconut, a pound of confetti, and a very thirsty yak. What they do may be very beautiful and spiritual and fulfilling, but it's not necessarily something you'd care to explain to a child. Okay, I think we've defined our terms, so let's get on with the explanation.

If you're nervous about explaining sex to a child, a good technique is to imagine that the child is not a child but is instead an alien from another planet. If it makes it easier for you, paint the child green and put a fake eye on its forehead. When the child asks you about sex, you can then say, "That sounds like English, but it's probably some weird alien language I'll never be able to understand. You're probably asking me to take you to my leader."

So you take the child to Washington, D.C., and insist that the President meet with the child. Then the President can explain sex to the child. I mean, what else has the President got to do? On second thought, this might not be such a great technique.

Okay then, what you've got to do is just explain sex simply and to the point. You just say, "When you get older you're going to meet somebody that you really, really, really like. Well, if you're lucky you're going to like that person. Maybe you don't even like 'em a lot, but at least they don't bug you too much. Or, okay, it's, let's say, closing time at the bar—it's really late and you've been knocking down quite a few Rusty Nails. And you know how the lighting is at those bars. I mean, everybody looks good. But then the next morning you look at the person next to you, and you're like, 'Argghhhh! Help me!' "

Maybe it's better to be a bit more allegorical. Tell a little story. You could say that there's a Papa Bear and a Mama Bear. And the Mama Bear says, "Where is that Papa Bear? He hasn't been home in a long time. He says he's working late at the pretzel factory, but I don't believe that lying grizzly bastard." So she hires another bear to follow the Papa Bear—a Detective Bear (or, if you prefer, a detective goat—don't be afraid to add your own spin to the story).

Well, the Detective Bear shadows the Papa Bear for a week. Then he tells the Mama Bear that every night, after work, Papa Bear goes to the same hotel room in the Poconos. Well, Mama Bear decides that she's going to give Papa Bear a big surprise. So, she goes to the hotel, kicks down the door, and there in the heart-shaped tub, sipping champagne, as naked as the day they were born are . . . No, this isn't a good way either.

There is a big fat queen Bee, and she likes her honey. So, she's in her hive and all these male bees are just buzzing around saying, "Oooo baby, I feel lucky tonight."

Or you take a big tub of butter, some milk, two or three eggs, a dash of vanilla . . . No, I'm sorry, that's not sex, that's my recipe for French toast. At least I hope that's not sex.

You know, I think the best idea is just to let the child watch cable TV. Or go out and rent 9½ Weeks. When I was in school, they showed us a sex education film about a boy calling up a girl on the phone and asking her out on a date. Nowadays, I'm sure they show 9½ Weeks or something starring Sharon Stone.

So, in conclusion, that's how I would talk to a child about sex. I sincerely hope that I've been of help. Excuse me, but I've got to go out for a short walk. All of a sudden it has gotten very hot in here, and I've developed a craving for French toast.

in the kitchen with ellen

or ....

as tasty as poison and just as deadly

How did people ever figure out that eggs were edible?

When I wasn't famous, nobody cared about how I ate or how I cooked or how I did my laundry or how I communicate telepathically with animals. But ever since becoming well known through my appearances on television, people seem to be a lot more curious about those things. Seems kind of funny to me, but, hey, if the public wants to know some of these things, I don't think I have the right not to tell them.

Well, I guess I do have the right to not tell. I mean, there's no law that says any person of famous or semifamous stature or reputation shall find it incumbent upon said person or personage to divulge eating, cooking, laundry, or animal-telepathy habits to the general public at large, or even in small groups. This is strictly a matter of choice for me, and I choose to say, "Yes. Yes, I *will* tell you what you want to know about me." And one of the things you seem to want to know most about me is my recipe for French toast.

It is one of my favorite recipes, and I bet dollars to donuts that after you try it out, it will be one of your favorites, too. Come to think of it, I'm not exactly sure I know what the saying "betting dollars to donuts" means. Maybe it used to be "betting donuts to donuts," but then . . . no, that still doesn't make sense. I don't even know when people started betting donuts. I do know that if you're in Las Vegas, you can't just go up to the roulette table, put a jelly donut on number 17, and shout out, "C'mon. Mama needs a big mess o' crullers!!" Believe me, I've tried. Oddly enough, you can put a chip down on any number. But it's a plastic chip and not the kind that you eat. So maybe it isn't all that odd after all.

But I digress.

Anyway, this is something that I cook up whenever people drop by, whether it's invited guests (Gus, my mailman), or tour buses filled with screaming fans (who tell me that I serve better food than Kevin Costner or Madonna).

Believe it or not, Ellen's Real Frenchy French Toast is also a great alternative to candy for trick or treaters on Halloween. Ah, the look on the little children's faces when I drop the still-steaming hot bread into their bags followed by a generous dollop of butter and a splash of maple syrup. You can see their faces because in Hollywood children don't wear masks on Halloween. They usually dress up as agents, valet parkers, or second-unit directors instead.

Now, on with the recipe.

Ingredients
BREAD
"What kind of bread should I use?!" you might say, panicking a wee bit early. Well, there are many types of bread: wheat, rye, white, Italian, Swiss, Dopey, Doc, pumpernickel . . . Do you know if you took every type of bread there is and laid them end to end—and I'm not counting crackers—well . . . Sorry, I'm not exactly sure of the point I'm trying to make. Maybe, just that it would go really really really far.

In the 1960s, bread was slang for money, as in "Hey, man, gimme some bread so I can buy a psychedelic headband." I don't know why that was. Maybe it's because in the 1940s, dough was slang for money, as in "Excuse me, Mister, can I borrow some dough so that I may purchase a spiffy fedora." One theory is that dough rose and eventually became bread. My point being that you shouldn't put money into this recipe.

EGGS
How did people ever figure out that eggs were edible? Did they see something come out of a chicken and think, "Boy, I bet that would be tasty?" There had to be a first person who ever ate an egg. I'm sure it wasn't pleasant. In fact, there are pictures in a cave in the south of France showing a Neanderthal crunching

into an egg and getting a big mouthful of egg shells, to the side there are other Neanderthals pointing at him and laughing. But who got the last laugh? I don't really know, I wasn't there. Also, this might not be true. It's possible it's just a dream I had one night after eating a bad clam.

People probably started eating some foods because they saw other animals eating them first. For instance, somebody saw a pig digging up truffles and eating them and said, "Say, that pig must know what he's doing. Otherwise he wouldn't be a pig. Hey, I can talk. Listen, everybody, I've invented language."

There had to be a first person who ate beets. Why why why didn't that person tell everybody that it wasn't worth the bother? To this day, people are still eating huge forkfuls of beets and asking God in Heaven how anybody decided that this could be food. Or, maybe that's just me.

SQUID
Actually there is no squid in this recipe. I was just thinking about them. I wonder what happened during their evolution to allow them to shoot out ink behind them. Some people think they developed this talent to avoid predators. But maybe it's just a neat magic trick: the squid squirting out the ink and when the ink disperses, the squid is gone. He's like the David Copperfield of the ocean. I'm not saying that a squid is married to a supermodel like Claudia Schiffer, but I'm not saying that he isn't, either.

BUTTER
If you have a moral or health reason for not using butter, then you can substitute some other lubricant, such as margarine, oil, or Vaseline. In a pinch you can rub a peanut really hard and fast over your pan. I've never tried this, but it's possible that you could squeeze out a drop or two of oil.

I probably should have mentioned earlier that you are going to need a . . .

PAN
You probably are also going to need a . . .

KITCHEN
I suppose you could cook the French toast over a heat source not found in a kitchen. You could try the cable box over your TV, but that doesn't give off much heat. It might take a year or two to cook the Real Frenchy French Toast properly. The same holds true for a candle. You'd need seventy or eighty candles to do the job right. You'd have to wait for your Uncle Hank's birthday party and cook over his cake. But, if you're doing this, you're just being obstinate. Go to the kitchen, use the stove, and stop being such a big baby.

SALT AND PEPPER (TO TASTE)
If you can't taste it, then it ain't salt and pepper! That's an old cooking joke. For the life of me, I've never been able to figure out what it meant.

VANILLA
If you don't have vanilla, you can substitute chocolate, butter pecan, or fudge ripple.

LAIT
That's french for milk. Calling it lait is what makes ordinary French toast Real Frenchy French Toast. You could call all of the ingredients by their french names, but then you'd run the danger of making Really Pretentious Frenchy French Toast.

To Cook
Now, do what I do. Give all the ingredients to your house-keeper, sit down with a . . .

COLD FROSTY BEER
in front of the TV, and before you can say Gerard Depardieu,   85
your housekeeper will be bringing out a piping hot bushel of
the tastiest French toast you've ever had.

Now, enjoy and bon appétit.

things that
sound like a
good idea at
first, but
really aren't

....

A. Taking a shower with someone.

B. Pet sitting.

C. Pie eating contests.

D. A mud bath followed by a shiatsu massage.

E. Having somebody read to you.
    1. Reading to someone else.

F. Writing a book.

ellen degeneres is a man!

or ....

ellen degeneres is a man!

WARNING!!!

ANOTHER POEM

I wish I were taller
And had perfect legs
And had easier hair to fix
And was a man
Sometimes I do
But not really
But sometimes
But not a lot
Just a little
Once in a while
O.K. only once
When I had to use the restroom
And somebody was in the ladies' room so it was locked
And the men's was open but I was too chicken to go in
So I wished I was a man then
Just that one time

Someone recently wrote a letter recently to a national magazine recently (and you know it must really be recently since I've mentioned it so many times) asking, "Why does Ellen DeGeneres always wear pants and never skirts?"

I'm guessing that the person who wrote that letter meant skirt, a noun signifying an article of clothing, and not skirt, a verb defined as, "to evade or elude (as a topic of conversation) by circumlocution." Because, if they mean the *verb* skirt, well, they're dead wrong. I'm always skirting. I skirt so much that it would not be inappropriate for someone to call me Skirty, though I can guarantee that I will never answer to that nickname.

But it's probably pretty safe to assume that the person who wrote that letter wanted to know why instead of wearing skirts, I wear pants.

First, let me just say, Wow! Some people have a lot of free time! I mean, it's one thing to wonder that to yourself. But to actually take time to write to a magazine about it? I have to conclude, however, that if one person wondered that, probably others have too. So, once and for all, here's the reason.

If you must know, years ago when I was young and impressionable, after eating some fermented berries at Camp Tatchey-Too Too, I had both my legs completely tattooed with designs of bougainvillaea. Now, if I wear a skirt, I am constantly bothered by bees.

I hope that clears that up. Thank you for your curiosity.

All kidding aside—actually, I change my mind. I don't want to put all kidding aside. I want the kidding right there in front where we all can see it. The main point of this book is kidding. If I put all kidding aside, there would be nothing left but nonkidding, and believe me, that wouldn't make a very interesting book. So forget that: the kidding stays (or I go).

Now, where was I? Oh yeah. Some people probably think that you're less of a woman if you wear pants, and that's just not fair (unless you're a man, in that case you might like being thought of as less than a woman . . . or at least less womanly —or maybe not). So, what am I trying to say? Probably something about how unfair it is to be judged by appearances. Yeah, that sounds right.

It is unfair to be judged by appearances. Even though I don't wear skirts, I know I'm a girl. Of course, I forget that sometimes. Wait a minute, I should clear that up. I can already see some reviewer singling that quote out. I don't forget that I'm a girl—I know I'm a girl (I've got two x chromosomes and I'm not afraid to use them)—but I think of myself as a human being first, just a person.

I'm a person who's a woman, and I don't like dresses or panty hose or heels. I guess you could chuckle and say that I'm just a woman trapped in a woman's body. But, if you did say that, nobody would know what you meant, and probably more than one person would ask you to kindly stop chuckling.

High heels should be outlawed (at the very least there should be a five-day waiting period before you can buy them). They destroy your feet. It should be mandatory that the Surgeon General print a warning label on high heels like they do on a package of cigarettes (i.e., Warning: These shoes can lead to lower back pain, aching toes, and the illusion that you're taller than you actually are).

Anyway, just to reiterate, I do know I'm a girl. As proof (and I don't know why you want proof all of a sudden), when I'm out in public and I have to use the restroom, I head straight for the ladies' room or the door with a stick figure wearing a dress (even though I'm not wearing one myself) or, if it's a seafood restaurant, the door marked "Gulls" and not "Buoys."

I guess the bigger point, though, is that fairly or unfairly (and sometimes both at the same time), we are judged by the way we look. And, more often than not, we're the ones who are judging ourselves.

I'm sometimes—by which I mean most of the time—insecure about the way I look. But, then again, I believe most people are insecure about their looks (though I'm not sure enough of myself to ask them). I'd bet even supermodels sometimes look at themselves in the mirror and say, "Oh, look. There's a part of me that's less perfect than the other parts of me that are more perfect."

I know that I'm being too critical. I know that I should just accept the way I look. I know that my appearance isn't as important to me as my thoughts and creativity and energy and relationships with people: that's what I thrive on. But none of this knowledge stops me from spending hours in front of the mirror looking for what I've been told (by the people waiting in line behind me at the Gap) are imaginary imperfections.

Doesn't it seem that when you look in the mirror, the tiniest imperfections seem huge? And you know that that's all people are going to be staring at all day: a blemish, a rebel strand of hair that refuses to behave, a flaming arrow in your forehead (this may not be a good example of a tiny imperfection).

So that I don't spend most of my day looking in the mirror consumed with self-doubt, I've developed some basic grooming and fashion tips that help me get started each day. And, on the small chance that they may help you, too, here they are.

There is only one rule: You've got to have nice shoes—that'll get you by. (Remember the saying: "I felt bad because I had no shoes, then I saw someone with really ugly shoes?") Well, unless you're wearing ratty old socks with holes in them. That would be stupid. So, nice shoes *and* nice socks are all you need.

And, of course there's your hair. That's important, too. It should be well-groomed—be it long or short. Here's another tip: If you've ever had spaghetti in your hair, you know it's hard to tell because, of course, it's long and stringy. Now if your hair *isn't* long and stringy, it's easier to tell. But, just in case, always check your hair every morning for spaghetti.

Any type of pasta aside, your hair should be trimmed regularly and have a clean, fresh appearance. Well, that goes for your overall body really—it should be clean and fresh. You should try to not have any perspiration (or very little) and smell good. Nice odor is important.

Now makeup, in my humble opinion, is optional. But that's just me. I've *never* understood the concept—except in movies and TV, where without makeup you look like a zombie; though, not enough like a zombie to get away without wearing any if you're playing a zombie in a movie. It's what we in L.A. call a vicious circle. Or maybe it's something else we call a vicious circle. Either way, makeup is optional.

Why must women wake up and paint their faces? Who came up with this idea? What's wrong with washing and moisturizing? So, if you wash and moisturize, if you care to wear makeup, go right ahead. No one's stopping you. I only suggest reconsidering. Is it totally necessary? If you are a man the same rule applies. Also if you care to shave, go ahead and shave.

So, now that the grooming part is taken care of, we'll move on to clothing. I won't go so far as to pick out your outfits, but they should be stylish—not trendy—classic clothes. They should be comfortable, not stifling or too conservative. Hats are optional, although it's a risk. It is definitely making a strong statement that others may react negatively to. So bear that in mind, won't you? Also remember, you're eventually going to take off your hat. And, there's no telling what your hair is going to look like. It may have given up hope and be lying dead on your scalp. Or, craving oxygen, it might be jutting out in surreal spikes. There may also have been spaghetti in your hat before you put it on. In that case, go back to the earlier tip.

Speak clearly and directly in an even tone, loud enough to be heard but not so loud as to be annoying. Have you put on those good shoes? Now you're ready for the day.

And remember, don't let anyone—not me, not even the great pasta chefs of Europe!—tell you how you *should* look.

97

chapter 13

See Chapter 14.

chapter 14

Regarding Chapter 13: I realized it's bad luck to have a thirteenth anything. Most hotels don't even have a thirteenth floor —they just go from twelve to fourteen. But you realize that fourteen is actually thirteen, so what good does it do? You can't eliminate the actual floor—it is, after all, thirteen—but they call it fourteen. So we all know that this is really Chapter 13 even though it says Chapter 14. I think I'll skip this one, too, and go on to Chapter 15, which will really then be fourteen.

the scariest thing

....

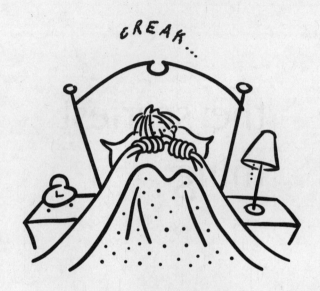

Whoever started all
those boogeyman stories
is a horrible person.

Real Fears vs. Ridiculous Fears

Fear of earthquakes.	Fear of a pack of wild baby kittens dropping on your head as you are sleeping soundly in your bed at night.
Fear of flying.	Fear of losing control of the volume of your speech while saying something rude about someone sitting in front of you while at church.
Fear of speaking in public.	Fear of combing your hair so hard your head bleeds while your date is waiting in the front room.
Fear of high places.	Fear of having the uncontrollable urge of shaving not only your head, but the heads of everyone you meet.
Fear of dying.	Fear of eating way too many oranges for no apparent reason.

When you're a grown-up and you're up really late, it's still scary, isn't it? No matter how much you try to convince yourself it's cool, it's okay, you're imagining those little noises. It's scary. Whoever started all those boogeyman stories is a horrible person. It had to be started, obviously, by one guy—one guy telling a little kid a bedtime story. He just threw in the boogeyman. Clearly it caught on. I doubt there are royalties involved—if there are, he's probably feeling ripped off. Who knew it would turn out to be such a big hit? Maybe he could try to sue K.C. and the Sunshine Band. Although it's a different boogeyman, the song still scares me. Don't get me wrong—I danced to it just as much as the rest of you in 1975—but come on, someone sat down and wrote those lyrics. But I digress. My point . . . and I do have one, is that I still get scared at night. Every tiny creak, every little noise, I open my eyes real wide and listen with them. Have you noticed that? When it's dark and you can't see a thing, you open your eyes really wide and glance back and forth, like your eyes become your ears? Maybe it's just me.

You can tell a lot about a person by looking at the things that scare her or him (actually, I'm not really sure that's true, but since it's the premise of this story, I'll write it down and hope that nobody reads it too carefully). Sometimes what a person fears is actually the thing that they desire. For instance, if somebody is afraid of ice cream it could mean that they desire ice cream (hence the saying, I scream, you scream, we all scream for ice cream). However, if that person is allergic to ice cream, it probably means that they desire hives or some other type of rash.

Some people believe that it's a good idea to face your fears. I usually feel that it's much healthier to tie them up in a bag, drive out to the country, chuck them out your window, then drive home as fast as you can. But at the moment, I'm lying in bed in the middle of the night. I'm too tired to take a long drive. So, I will try looking into my heart to see what frightens me.

Ghosts. I'm afraid of ghosts. Do I really believe in ghosts?

Sometimes I do. I watch these supernatural phenomenon shows about people who have seen doors and windows open and close and furniture move around the room. Sometimes I think, "Cool, I'd love to see that." But, most of the times, I wouldn't. I'd get kind of freaked out if a coffee table started dancing around, even if it was a goofy dance like the hokey-pokey.

The house I live in now might have a ghost. I think I've seen the guy. When I first moved into this house, strange things happened. I'd lock a door and a few minutes later I'd see that it was unlocked. A sliding door opened. It could've been the wind, you say. Well then, my skeptical friend, explain why there was a man standing in the middle of my bedroom dressed in some turn-of-the-century attire. Actually, it turns out that the man was my neighbor who got lost coming home from a costume party at Ernest Borgnine's house. But it could have been a ghost.

I'm also afraid of space aliens and spaceships. I'm scared that I'll be abducted by some UFO and then poked and prodded, which, from what I read, is what space aliens mostly do. Or what if they put some sort of chip in your brain that made you kill at their command or, even worse, made your favorite radio station the easy-listening one? What would be frightening, then, would be to come back and know that if you told anyone what happened to you, they'd think you were a nut. The only thing that scares me more than space aliens is the idea that there aren't any space aliens. We can't be the best that creation has to offer. I pray we're not all there is. If so, we're in big trouble.

Let's see, what else frightens me. Oh, I know. The scariest thing in the world almost happened to me the other day. Just thinking about it makes me break into a sweat (or maybe it's the hour and a half that I just spent on my treadmill that has caused me to break into a sweat; the important thing is that I'm sweating). Let me tell you about it. But first, a warning: If you are faint of heart, it would be a good idea to have a registered nurse nearby while you read this tale of near-terror. On the other hand, if you are a registered nurse, there's no need to have a faint-of-heart person with you. All they'd do is fidget around a lot and make you nervous.

I was at home, I was barefoot, I was about to put my shoes on . . . (Have I set the mood, is your heart beating fast?) Like a fool, I was just going to slip my foot into my shoe without looking. Luckily, at the last second I glanced down. In my shoe was . . . a huge spider—a big black-and-orange, hairy, crunchy spider. I almost put my foot right on it. Isn't that scary? Isn't that like something Stephen King would write? Stepping on a spider has to be the scariest thing in the world.

Actually, do you know what would be scarier? If, after putting on the one shoe I then recklessly put my foot in the other only to discover that it was teeming with . . . *hundreds* of spiders! All the babies were in there, a whole—let's see, it's a gaggle of geese, a school of fish, what is a group of spiders called? Oh, now I remember: a whole *snorkel* of spiders. That would be the scariest thing ever.

Unless, let's say you're out camping in the woods, or not even camping, or even in the woods; you're sleeping in your backyard. I don't know why. Maybe you like the great outdoors, but you want to be close to home in case somebody calls. Or maybe you had a fight with the person you live with, and you ended up yelling, "Okay, that does it. I'm sleeping in the backyard tonight!" It's only when you get back there that you realize it wasn't much of a threat. But you have too much pride to go and sleep inside (even though your dogs look at you from inside through the picture window with an expression that's a mixture of pity and confusion).

So (and this is the scary part), you're in the backyard and you're just about to doze off when you start feeling something kind of funny—not ha ha funny, but creepy, weird funny. So you look inside your sleeping bag and there's . . . a snake crawling up your leg. Aghhhhhhh! That just blows the spider thing away. It is not possible for there to be anything scarier than that.

Wait, I just thought of something more frightening. What if you're playing Frisbee on the beach and the person you're playing with (either a friend or someone kind of attractive who just happens to have a Frisbee, and you're flattered when they ask you to play with them—this part isn't important so you shouldn't be dwelling on it) throws the Frisbee way past you and you're furious because it's their fault, but you smile and yell, "I'll get it," and they say, "Okay." (Notice how I've managed to build up the suspense with some terse dialogue?)

Anyway, it turns out that the Frisbee has flown into one of those caves that you see at most beaches. Well, you go to get it and you realize that the Frisbee has gone farther down into that cave than you had thought. So you have to spelunk down into the abysmal depths of the pitch-black cave.

Finally, you reach what you assume is your Frisbee and you grab it, but it feels weird so you say, "Why is my Frisbee squishy?" So you squeeze it harder and you realize, "Hey, this isn't a Frisbee . . . it's a bat!"

Well, the bat starts making that *wee-bee-bee-bee* bat noise that bats make when you're squeezing them a little too hard (for more information on this read *Bats and the Sounds They Make When You Squeeze Them*, by Carney Pheek). So you start running as fast as you can out of the cave, but your screaming sets off thousands of bats—not a snorkel, that's only for spiders—a whole *Nipsy Russell* of bats, which start flying out after you. Now you're running through the sand, which is even harder than it sounds because you're wearing high heels (they look good with the swimsuit and slenderize your hips). So you're heading for the water thinking you'll be safe from the bats. But just before you submerge, a bat bites you on the ear. Oh man, those sharks can smell blood from miles away. So now you can see the shark fins swimming toward you. But you can't get out of the water because of the Nipsy Russell of bats. What a dilemma. It's like *The Pit and the Pendulum*, only different. I defy you to come up with something scarier than that. It's impossible.

Unless, say you're on a farm visiting your aunt . . . or whomever . . . and she calls out to you through the kitchen window, "Ellen, Ellen honey—would you mind going to look for that thing I misplaced?" And you don't even care what the thing is—because that guy's inside and he wants you to call him Uncle Larry and he's not your uncle and he's drunk all the time and he always wears those weird pajamas—but it's her life. So you go to look for that thing, and you think you see it in some bushes. You reach in to grab it, and you think you have it, but what you realize you're grabbing instead is (Oh my God!!!) a . . . lamb.

Okay, I admit that's not too scary by itself. But what if it's not just one lamb? What if it's a lot of lambs? What if it's a rack of lambs? That's pretty scary, huh? Because a lot of anything is scarier than one something.

Am I right? Think about it. One hundred poodles are scarier than one leopard. That's assuming, of course, that the leopard has no legs. You could come home, open the door, and see a leopard with no legs sitting in your living room. So what could it do? It's got no legs. It would be growling away, and you could sit right in front of it and make faces and touch its nose and "Woo" at it.

The only way a no-legged leopard could hurt you is if it fell out of a tree onto your head. I don't know how it got up the tree; maybe some of the other animals lifted it up there. But you have to admit when that leopard fell on you and clamped down on your head with its teeth, it would be pretty bad. You'd start running down the street yelling, "Help, help me, please."

And more often than not, you'd run into a big group of animal-rights activists, a *Naugahyde* of animal-rights activists. And, instead of helping, they'd probably throw red paint at you. You would scream out, "It's not a hat, it's a live animal! It's got no legs. I would never wear fur. I am wearing it against my will."

So now you've got a live leopard on your head and paint all over you as well. That is pretty darn terrifying. But you know, I don't want to diminish the spider in my shoe. Believe me, looking back, that was scary enough. I guess all I'm trying to say is you don't have to make stuff up; there are enough scary things in real life.

the time ellen degeneres had an emergency!

···

Just flap, flap, flapping
in the breeze...

Once I had to be taken to the emergency room of a hospital. It was an experience I wouldn't wish on my worst enemy. Actually, I don't have a worst enemy or even a best enemy. I've never taken the time to rank my enemies. I'm afraid of hurting somebody's feelings. "Hey, I thought I was your worst enemy," one of my lesser enemies might complain. I sort of wish I did have a worst enemy, though. Because, come to think of it, having them go to the emergency room is exactly the sort of thing that I would wish on them. I mean, what's the point of having a worst enemy if you can't take enjoyment from seeing them suffering and in pain? It would be kind of fun. As it was, it was me suffering and in pain.

I got hurt in a real stupid way. Before they tape my sitcom, I go out and warm up the audience a little bit. Usually I tell jokes, but sometimes I perform feats of strength. You know, like pulling a jeep across the stage using my teeth. Well, this time I had people come up from the audience; I would tense my stomach muscles and they'd punch me as hard as they could. Everything was going fine until I relaxed for just one second. Out of nowhere this huge teamster ran over from the donut table and socked me in the gut. It was either a teamster or Dom DeLuise dressed up like a teamster.

That's not really what happened. I just don't care to tell you why I really went to the emergency room. Okay, I had a cyst. See, it's not quite as interesting as getting socked in the gut by Dom DeLuise. But still, it did hurt like hell.

I was in bed doubled over in pain. It really confused my dogs. That's not saying much, though. It doesn't take a lot to confuse my dogs. Ringing the doorbell does the trick.

My manager, a man who told me that it was in my best interest that I don't know his name, so I refer to him always as "my manager," drove me to the hospital. I would have taken an ambulance, but when I called on the phone they told me that you had to book one two weeks in advance. It's just as well. I never know how much to tip the drivers of those things anyway.

We picked up my mother on the way. She wanted to come because that way we could ride in the car pool lane. Also, she works as a speech pathologist at the hospital I was going to. She figured since she was an employee she could make things easier for me. You know, like getting me a good table and giving me the skinny on how things work there. "You see that man in the white coat with a stethoscope? He's a doctor." (Thanks, Mom.) "If you were to speak to him you would call him Dr. Jones and not Mr. Jones. That is, assuming that his last name is Jones."

When you're in terrible pain, you don't care about the way you look; you're not embarrassed by your facial contortions and grimaces; you don't care if you're wearing plaids with stripes, which, thank God, I wasn't.

I was doubled over in the car, my face pressed against the window (the passenger window, not the front window), crying out in pain. When we were stopped at red lights, people would look over from the next car. They'd see my manager driving and me sitting next to him crying. You could see on their faces what they were thinking. First they'd think that I was in an abusive relationship and had just been hit. Then they'd slowly recognize me, honk their horns, and give me a big thumbs up. My manager would never hit me, but while I was groggy from the pain he did have me sign something that gives him 50 percent of whatever I make.

They rushed me into the emergency room: doors slamming, voices overlapping, people running—a flurry of activity. But as soon as I got in, I had to sit and wait and wait and wait. It's not fair. It's not like the bakery where you take a number and it's first come first served. Here they have this crazy idea of bringing you in based on how serious they feel your illness or injury is. I knew I was in for a long wait when I saw a guy sitting next to me with his arm falling off and his head in his lap. As it was, he was only there for the happy hour. If you're admitted between five and six there's a buffet table with cocktail franks and nachos.

The first thing I had to do, besides proving that I had insurance, was tell them what my symptoms were. Unfortunately, they recognized me as a comic, so they thought I was trying to be funny, that I was trying out a new part of my act.

I said, "I have this sharp intense pain in my lower abdomen. I started feeling it about two hours ago. . . ."

And the admitting nurse would interrupt me, barely able to control her giggling, "Yeah, yeah. . . . Then what happened? Wait! Mary, Stan, come over here, she's really funny. Start from the beginning."

"I was hurting so much I couldn't move," I continued.

The admitting nurse started laughing hysterically. "Oh yes. That's great, it's hilarious. Oooooo, I've got an idea. Tell the rest of it like you're on the phone with God. That would make it really funny."

So after I made it past the admitting nurse, they had me sit on these extremely uncomfortable plastic chairs (they were rejected by Greyhound bus stations for being too painful) in the waiting area again until they could find someone to help me. Everybody else there was watching TV. They finally wheeled me in to see a doctor because my crying and screaming in pain was ruining people's TV-viewing experience. "Keep it down, we're trying to watch Jerry Springer!"

They gave me a number of tests to try to figure out what was wrong: blood tests, X-rays, ultrasound, temperature, algebra. Some tests seemed valid; others seemed to serve no purpose at all. Like when one doctor had me sit on a pony and whistle the theme song from *Mission Impossible.* "Why do I have to do this?" I said between whistles.

"We just want to rule out whistling pony disease," he replied, "and anyway, Dr. Jones brought the pony in so we figured we might as well use it."

What was really bad was when this guy tried to hook me up to an IV. He kept on missing my vein. He'd stab at me and miss; there was blood everywhere. I got really nervous when I looked down and saw his Seeing Eye dog.

I told the nurse I didn't think this guy knew what he was doing and I'd prefer it if she put in the IV. She looked at me surprised. "I'm sorry, I thought you wanted him to do it. I have no idea who this guy is."

The doctor came in later. He said that my blood looked good and that my urine was clear and looked good too. That calmed me, until I realized that I hadn't even had a urine test. Either he had looked at somebody else's urine or he found me attractive and this was one of his pick-up lines. Maybe I was supposed to tell him that his urine was clear and looked good also.

I was tested until midnight. Everybody looked at me. At one point, a doctor's neighbor's nephew's son was examining me. If that isn't wacky, I don't know what wacky is. Eventually, by doing an ultrasound, they discovered that I had a cyst that the doctor said was the size of a really, really big cyst.

Finally, at midnight, I was wheeled into my hospital room. It was a little disappointing. No mint on the pillow, no view, no HBO. And believe me, this place wasn't cheap either.

Shortly afterward they brought me my first meal. Now the food in hospitals is the stuff that's so bad that it doesn't even make it onto airplanes. They brought me broth and Jell-O, which ironically is one of my favorite meals. If it's fixed right, it's great. I think it's bad when broth and Jell-O taste exactly the same.

Another thing that's awful is the gown they make you wear. It doesn't fit right, and it's completely open in the back, leaving exposed an area of my body that I traditionally keep covered with clothes. You walk down the hall and it's just flap, flap, flapping in the breeze—the gown, that is; the part of my body I traditionally keep covered wasn't flap, flap, flapping. If it was, I'm sure I'd be one of the first people to know. All I'm saying is that the gown was humiliating. But, on the bright side, since the hospital is in Beverly Hills, my gown also had shoulder pads. So, it was slimming and degrading at the same time. I think Cher wore one to the Oscars last year.

I was depressed when I woke up the next morning. Because besides being sick, it was my birthday. There's nothing like spending your birthday hooked up to an IV and trying to keep your gown closed in the back to make you aware of the aging process, the inevitability of death and decay, and countless other happy, carefree thoughts.

They did cheer me up, though, when they brought me my breakfast: broth and Jell-O. Somebody must have known it was my birthday because they put a candle in the broth.

It wasn't my worst birthday, though. That would have to be either the year I decided to eat my age in hard-boiled eggs, the year I thought I had gotten tickets to see the musical *Tommy* but instead ended up seeing a one-man show based on the life of Tom Bosley, or when I turned twelve and fell off my pony while whistling the theme from *Mission Impossible*.

On the other hand, I did lose five pounds a lot quicker than I would have by dieting, and I had someone cute tell me that my urine looked good.

Luckily I was able to go home after just one day. But I had

to rest for a long time. We lost a week of production on my show. And, to be honest, the first week or two that I was back I don't think we made the best episodes. My character was always lying in bed with her feet slightly elevated. Every now and then they would cut to me and I would just react to whatever action was taking place and say something like: "Wow, that's crazy" or "You don't say" or "You learn something new every day, don't you?"

It was heartwarming going back to the set for the first time after recuperating. Everybody was so happy to see me. Well, everybody but Erik Estrada. He had been promised my role if I didn't make it back and had already started rehearsing. I think it would be a completely different show, him playing Ellen instead of me. I'm not saying worse, just different.

The whole experience of being sick and going to the emergency room has really made me value how good life is without a cyst. It has also made me appreciate the little things in life. Like . . . Actually, I can't think of anything right now. All that popped into my head was "mashed potatoes." And, well, I like mashed potatoes, but I can't honestly say I appreciate them more than I ever did. Oh, I guess I do appreciate having clothes that aren't open in the back.

On the down side—if there can be a down side to having a ruptured cyst—I'm now much more of a hypochondriac than I ever was. For instance, just the other day I was sure that I had an awful stomach ulcer. It turned out that I had just left one of the pins in my new blouse.

So, my advice to everybody reading this is simple: Don't have a cyst. Believe me, it's not all the fun and kicks it's made out to be.

one step
closer to god

or ....

one step back,
you do the hokey-pokey
and you turn yourself around

Hey, what's a matter,
were you born in a barn?

Like most of us humans (if you're a nonhuman and are another species of animal instead, like a llama, screech-monkey, or whatever, then congratulations on learning how to read), I am always searching for answers. Sometimes I don't even know the question, and yet I need answers. Sometimes I know the answer and I need the question, but that's only when I'm watching *Jeopardy*.

Some of the answers I search for are to questions like: What is the meaning of life? How did it all begin? Is there such a thing as infinity? (It boggles my mind that there is no beginning or end to the universe, only a big middle that's probably the result of too much starchy foods.) Now, don't get the wrong idea. I don't think about this stuff constantly. Sometimes I just sit in my den and watch *Wheel of Fortune*. That Vanna White sure seems like a sweet girl—so happy and upbeat.

But right now I am thinking about those big questions, because right now I'm thinking about God. That's because there's a woman, who by the looks of her is either from India or Sweden, about one hundred yards away from me (I say one hundred because I'm sitting under one field goal and she's under another, so I'm guessing one hundred). She has been sitting on a tree stump rocking back and forth with little beads and a tiny book in her hands for two hours—praying sort of out loud. I can't really hear what she's saying, but man oh man, two hours? What could you possibly pray about for two hours?

I'd like to tell her, "Excuse me, Miss, but he's busy—or she or whoever. Keep it short. There are people in Yemen who would like to talk."

I think that when you pray, it's like you're leaving a message for God. You don't want to have God check her answering machine, hear your rambling prayer, and say, "Two hours, two hours?! There will be no time for miracles today. That's for darn sure."

I try to keep my prayers simple, like: "Hey, God, what's up? Thanks for everything in my life. I'm so grateful. Thanks especially for helping me find that parking space today. That was sweet of you. Hope you're doing okay. Sorry for the mess we're making here blah, blah, blah." (I literally say, blah, blah, blah— don't ask me why, it just feels good.) I'm finished in less than five minutes (saving God time so that she can have a personal life).

Sometimes when I'm driving I get so angry at inconsiderate drivers that I want to scream at them. But then I remember how insignificant that is, and I thank God that I have a car and my health and gas. That was phrased wrong—normally you wouldn't say, thank God I've got gas. I meant gasoline for my car. But some people who have strange diseases may actually be thinking "Hey, if I only had gas, I'd feel lucky." So, like most things in life, it's all relative.

I was raised a Christian Scientist and was taught to believe that we could heal our bodies through prayer, that sickness was an illusion that could be defeated by the power of the spirit. Since my family were Christian Scientists, we probably saved a bundle: no aspirin, no medicine at all. I didn't take my first aspirin until I was in my teens and even now I feel a twinge of guilt when I go to the pharmacy—I feel as if I'm in an opium den. (Though, to be fair, I've only been to an opium den twice and I was so stoned I barely remember what it was like.) We never had to buy any of that stuff. Also, we didn't need medical insurance. It would have been a waste of money because we never went to the hospital.

I don't recall much about my religious upbringing. I remember I wore a bonnet to church, but I don't think it was a Chris-

tian Science thing to wear bonnets. It was just me and maybe a
few other girls (and this guy named Owen who wore a bonnet
because he burned easily and was allergic to all other kinds of
hats).

Sometimes I wonder what God is like. We picture God to
look like us. Not exactly. I mean, I don't think we picture God   129
to look like Wink Martindale, for instance. More like Bob
Barker. But we assume God has some human form. Maybe God
looks more like those drawings of aliens that people have sup-
posedly seen with large heads and huge, black eyes. Maybe
God is a huge sphere with millions of ears or antennas like a
satellite dish for excellent reception. Maybe God is a giant bug,
and when we die we're going to have to account for every
cockroach and ant we've killed. Maybe God does look like
Wink Martindale.

I believe that there is a lot to be learned from the Bible. But I
don't believe all the stories can be taken literally. Because nobody was writing things down as they happened. Instead, one
person told somebody else, who then told someone else, who
told Shem, who told Hosea, who told Sinbad, who told Fabio,
who told somebody else. So, what started out as a story about
Moses going to the beach to get a little sun and maybe go
snorkeling became the Red Sea parting and all that stuff.

That being said, here are two of my favorite Bible stories:

God is in a department store and he asks a woman where
the hat section is. I don't remember the woman's name, so I'll
call her Linda, because I have a friend named Linda who works
in a department store. Now this story took place a long time
ago—when department stores had huge hat sections. I don't
remember what kind of hat God was looking for either. Proba-

bly something with a snap brim. So Linda tells God, "Go to the . . ." I'm sorry. Linda tells God *"Thou shall go* to the third floor. The hats are right next to the Laura Ashley accessories."

You know, that might not be a Bible story. It might just be a boring story that Linda told me once. (I think it was about her selling a scarf to Charles Nelson Reilly. I kept falling asleep, so I must have dreamed the God part.)

This, however, I'm pretty sure is a Bible story. Jesus enters the temple and he's steaming mad because there are money-lenders in there. I forget what they were doing, probably lending money. Well, Jesus turns over their tables and exits in a huff, leaving the door to the temple wide open. So, one of the moneylenders yells out, "Hey, what's a matter, Jesus, were you born in a barn?" Which is ironic, because he was.

Note: I wanted to put a story here that I used to do in my stand-up act about a phone call to God. It was a signature piece of mine, meaning that when I would sign a check I'd write out the entire routine instead of my name. It would take about a half hour, so it was usually better for other people to pay my bills.

The piece is very funny. I start off saying how I feel that everything on this earth is here for a reason, that there are no mistakes. If you don't understand why one thing is here, you find out later that it works with the ecosystem somewhere else. (In case you're wondering, this wasn't the funny part, this was just the setup.)

I went on to say that I don't understand why we have fleas here, because fleas do nothing at all beneficial. I thought it would be great to be able to call up God and ask, "Why fleas?"

What followed was my imaginary phone call to God. I would say my lines and hopefully you'd be able to imagine God's. God and I would chat, he'd tell me a few jokes (e.g., Knock, Knock. Who's there? God. God who? Godzilla), and explain to me why there are fleas (to support people in the flea-collar industry). This was the funny part. If you've never heard it, take my word: huge laughs every night.

So why aren't I writing it out here? There are two reasons. One, as funny as it is to see and hear (If you don't believe me, maybe this note from my editor will change your mind. EDITOR: *She's right, it's very funny!*) it doesn't read well on the page. So much of the routine depends on nuances of timing and my delightful facial expressions (EDITOR: *She's right, they're delightful*). (Why, thank you.)

The second reason is that I got a letter from God, well, actually from God's lawyers, saying that if I printed the routine, they'd sue my ass (their words, not mine) from here to Jerusalem.

So, that's why I'm not even going to mention my phone call to God.

the ellie-gellie

Cleanliness is next to
Godliness, but dancing is
next to cleanliness.

If you know me personally, or watch my television program, then you know I love to dance. I really do, y'all. (Y'all is a New Orleans expression that I felt obliged to include at least once in this book to show that I haven't "Gone Hollywood." There, I've used it. Now no highfalutin' critic can say that I've forgotten where I came from.)

Anyway, like I said, I love dancing. You know that expression, "Cleanliness is next to Godliness"? Well, I believe that, but *dancing* is next to cleanliness, and singing along to the radio in a convertible with the wind whipping through your hair is next to dancing, and walking down a country road at sunset is next to singing along with the radio with the wind whipping through your hair, and walking down a country road at dawn is next to walking down a country road at sunset. Actually one is virtually indistinguishable from the other, but the dawn one requires getting up really early, so I'd rather just walk down the country road at sunset, unless I had to be up anyway, say if I had to pick up an old friend from the airport or I had to take somebody to the hospital or even if I just couldn't sleep. Then I guess I'd prefer walking down that country road at dawn and just getting it over with.

I have a good dance background. I've probably got a more extensive dance background than a lot of people, just to tell you something about my skills. I rarely missed *Soul Train* while growing up. And although I was never actually what you might call "on" the show itself, my friends all said that I "could've been" if I hadn't been born quite so "white," as they put it.

Since I feel blessed in this area, I think it's only right that I share my gift with you, the people who may *not* have been born with the same sense of rhythm. I'm going to teach you a simple yet hip dance I invented. I call it the Ellie-Gellie.

Alrightee, first thing we have to do is get into our dance

gear. That could be a leotard, sweats, glittery tights, whatever . . .

Hey, I like that. It looks good on you, accentuates your body in just the right way. It'll work perfectly.

Next we need to do some stretching. . . . Good. You don't want to overdo it.

And now you'll need to send away for my song, "The Ellie-Gellie Song." I wrote it specifically to do the Ellie-Gellie to. It works better than any other song for this dance, and although you *can* do the Ellie-Gellie to some other song, I can't guarantee the results. And you'll probably look rather silly doing the Ellie-Gellie to another song.

But if looking asinine doesn't bother you, then, hey, it's your life, you're obviously Mr. or Ms. Big Stuff, so go right ahead. You probably can't dance anyway, so it wouldn't make any difference either way if you used "The Ellie-Gellie Song" or some other stupid song. I don't even know why I bother trying to do something nice for someone like you. Even if I *could* teach you the Ellie-Gellie, which I highly doubt, you'd probably screw it up while dancing at some club and everyone would see you and say, "Man, the Ellie-Gellie is really a bad dance. That Ellen DeGeneres is sure a terrible dance inventor." So, it's just as well that you don't send away for "The Ellie-Gellie Song." And if you did send away for it, I'd send your money back. You couldn't get my song now no matter *how much* you paid for it.

All right, everybody else except for that creep ready? . . . Good, let's get started. Hit *play* on the CD player, tape player, record player, or whatever kind of player you happen to be using, and crank up the volume!

Not quite that loud. Turn it down just a bit. . . . There, much better. Now we're ready to D-A-N-C-E!

First, throw your left arm up in the air and shake your head up and down, but not too much. Still too much . . . still too much . . . what are you, stupid? Stop all that ridiculous shaking! I said to shake your head *mildly!* . . . There, that's better.

Next, with arm still up in the air, do something with one of your legs. There, very good. I like that.

Now, do a *different* movement with the *other* leg. . . . No, no! What're you doing?! Is that supposed to be cool or sexy or something? You look like one of those big ol' ostriches at the zoo, flopping around all gangly and everything! Just stop it and start "The Ellie-Gellie Song" over again.

You know what? Just forget it. You've got me too riled up to be able to teach effectively now. Maybe I'll try it again in the next book. By then my nerves will be calmer, and I'll probably have several more dances for you to screw up.

See you on *Soul Train*!

137

things to do
if you're stuck
in an elevator
to help you
pass the time

1. Don't panic—being alone with yourself can be a healthy thing.

2. Try to whistle as many television theme songs as you can remember.

3. Think of your family—the ones you don't hate—and all of the fun times you've had.

4. Think of your favorite foods and how they are prepared (try not to think of corn on the cob or other foods that would require flossing).

5. Make pancakes (this only applies if you've got a hot plate, pancake mix, and an electrical outlet).

6. Count your arm hairs.

7. Think about giraffes giving birth and how they don't injure the baby when it drops.

8. Prepare your grocery lists for the year.

9. This is a perfect time to reflect on your childhood and who hurt you.

10. Scream.

ellen's wild kingdom

or ....

*you can put high heels on a
poodle, but that won't make it
a hooker*

I do believe that most
animal testing is improper.

KNOWN HORRIBLE EXPRESSIONS

1. Curiosity killed the cat.
2. No sense in beating a dead horse.
3. A bird in the hand is worth two in the bush.

LESS-KNOWN HORRIBLE EXPRESSIONS

1. Why put a weasel in the blender when you can chop it up by hand?
2. When you see a chipmunk, poke it in the eye—hard.
3. More than one way to file a kitten's tooth.

I went camping recently for the first time. It was a fantastic experience. I went to an amazing place: Montana. I don't know if you've been there, but it is gorgeous. I've never seen any place so spectacularly beautiful as Montana. Or was it Maine? It *was* Maine. Anyway, it is beautiful, and I've never seen any place like it. It is so special.

The important thing is that I went camping. Now, I normally don't wake up that early, but I woke up to watch the sun set. I was sitting in front of my tent, and eating breakfast—some type of Mueslix, or some other kind of outdoorsy stuff, just eating it right from my hand. I didn't even have a bowl. I just had milk and the Mueslix and my hand.

Anyway, so I'm enjoying my Mueslix (That may be an exaggeration—let's just say I was *eating* my Mueslix), when suddenly I hear some kind of noise. Since I'm alone in the middle of the woods, I'm a little bit scared. But I gather my courage, look up, and . . . Awww, how cute! Only ten feet away from where I'm sitting there's a family of deer drinking from a little, babbling brook thing (I'm not sure of the technical outdoorsy term). Just the mother, father, and two little baby deer lit by the reddish glow of the setting sun. It was so beautiful, so perfect, so wonderful, and I thought, "Oh, I wish I had a gun." I could've just . . . *BANG BANG BANG BANG BANG!* I could have shot 'em, gutted 'em, skinned 'em, then sprinkled 'em on my cereal.

Actually, none of that story is true. Well, some of it is true. I did go camping in Maine.

No, that's not true either. The closest I've come to camping in Maine is spending a few nights at the Hilton in Maui (come to think of it, that's not very close). My point . . . and I do have one, is that I was being sarcastic. I don't understand hunting at all.

My cousin Archie is into hunting, and he knows that I hate it, but that just makes him want to talk about it to me more. He called me the other day and said, "You should've seen it, Ellie. Heh, heh, heh. I got myself an eight-point duck." Well, I don't know the terminology, but it was something like that.

Archie told me all the details, ending with him dragging the deer up to his car. Luckily, he got his license back; before, he would have had to drag it up to the highway and hitchhike. Not many people will pick up a man and a deer—maybe one or the other, but not both.

All through Archie's story all I could think about was that poor little innocent animal just standing around thinking little deer thoughts: "I wonder where the berries are. What's this on my hoof?" Whatever they're thinking. Then Archie killed him and put his head (the deer's, not Archie's) on the wall of his living room. "Heh, heh, heh, heh, heh. I shot it. Heh, heh, heh. I killed it. No, it wasn't doing anything to me, just standing there. What's your point?"

I can see if it was something that you hated, just something that you were so proud that you killed. Like a burglar. Get his last expression of surprise before you shot him. "Heh, heh, heh, heh, heh. Shot him. Heh, heh. I killed him. He was coming in. Going for the Sony."

I ask people why they have deer heads on their walls, and they say, "Because it's such a beautiful animal." There you go. Well, I think my mother's attractive, but I have *photographs* of her. "Wasn't Mom pretty? She had great legs, too. They're in the next room, come on."

I tell you, the deer heads that I feel sorry for the most are the ones on the walls of bars or restaurants. They have the silly party hats on them, silly sunglasses, streamers around their necks. These are the ones I feel sorry for. I mean, obviously, they were at a party having a good time. They were in there dancing to their little deer music, "A crossbow will make ya *JUMP—JUMP!*" Then, all of a sudden . . . *ker-plow!* . . . the party's over.

Now, I don't want you to get the wrong idea. I'm a strong supporter of animal rights, but I do feel that some activists go a little bit too far. For instance, going up to Alaska and throwing paint at the Eskimos because of the fur coats they wear seems wrong to me. Some activists even eliminate the middleman; they throw paint right on the animal itself (I suppose that would really be the middlemink and not the middleman). The activist says to the mink, "Why wait? You're going to end up on somebody eventually." But the mink is still pissed off, "Hey! I just had a bath. How am I going to get this red paint off? And don't go telling me about club soda—that won't work."

I do believe, though, that most animal testing is improper. If you want to test cosmetics, why do it on some poor animal who hasn't done anything wrong? They should use prisoners who have been convicted of murder or rape instead. So, rather than seeing if some perfume irritates a bunny rabbit's eyes, they should throw it in Charles Manson's eyes and ask him if it hurts.

Another type of animal testing that I think is really wrong is having animals take the SATs. Their scores are always so low, and it's just not fair. It makes them feel stupid, but that's only because the tests are biased toward humans. Because if you asked a person if some type of food is edible, they might not know. They'd eat it and die. An animal wouldn't do that. But if you asked a dog, "Egg is to nest as baby is to what?" it would just stare at you. Or maybe bite your leg. Or go to the bathroom on your carpet. They feel so depressed afterward, because they just don't know. You give them their score, and they just look and say, "Huh?" Then you have to say, "I'm sorry, Mr. Doggy, but you can't go to Harvard."

Even though the animals we share this earth with don't do well on standardized tests (partially, I think, because it's hard to fill in the circles completely with their little paws), they do have an intelligence and beauty that is all their own. It's inspiring to me to be with them, watch them, and try to understand them.

So, I went to the zoo today . . . maybe it was yesterday . . . or last year. It's hard to tell when you're writing a book. I mean, I could have gone to the zoo today, but you could be reading this five years from now. You might read this same page every day for a month and think, "That's odd. Every time I read this page, Ellen says she went to the zoo. That means she's gone to the zoo every day for thirty days in a row. Boy, she must really like the zoo. Come to think of it, I must really like this page. I mean, why else would I be reading it every day for a month? I either like this page a lot or I'm going insane. Maybe I should see a doctor. Maybe I already have seen a doctor. I'm hungry. I think I'll fix myself a sandwich."

Anyway, at the zoo they're very proud about how they've

managed to re-create the animal's natural habitat. I'm not exactly sure who "they" are. I just know that "they" hang around the zoo, wear funny hats, and tell everyone how proud "they" are that the zoo has re-created the animals' natural habitat. And, I must admit, the zoo has done a great job. I'm sure I've seen in those Jane Goodall chimpanzee documentaries plenty of tires on ropes swinging from trees in the jungle. And who can visualize a pride of lions on the Serengeti without imagining cages, moats, and little kids throwing marshmallows at the lions? I know I can't. Also, most animals get real ornery if they don't smell cotton candy, the natural odor of the wild.

You've got to wonder what the animals think in a zoo. The first day at school is bad enough; imagine your first day in a zoo. All these strange species staring at you, and you're saying, "What are they looking at? Is there something on my lip? Hey, you see I'm locked up; get me out of here!" I'm sure some animals go crazy in captivity and crack. "Hey, it wasn't me. It was some other polar bear who looked like me. Let me out and I'll help you find him and we can beat the crap out of him."

A lot of times at the zoo you see the monkeys throwing their own poop. I don't blame them. It must be so boring in there, you've got to do something to entertain yourself. I mean all that's there is a tire, a tree, and a few bananas. If I were in the zoo, I'm sure eventually I'd be throwing my poop. (I'm misquoted so often in the press that I'm sure this will be the one paragraph taken out of context in the reviews of this book. The headline will probably be: ELLEN WANTS TO THROW HER OWN POOP. Oh, well.)

I bet they get sick of the food they're served, too. I can just imagine some monkey saying, "Man, they see us eating bananas once and they figure that's *all* we want to eat. Geez, would it kill them to give us some Chee-tos, a ham sandwich, or some cotton candy?"

It makes me especially sad to see dolphins in captivity, because they are such incredibly smart animals. That doesn't mean that I'd want a dolphin to perform brain surgery on me. It has less to do with intelligence than one, I don't want anyone performing brain surgery on me and two, dolphins don't have any hands. It is very hard to hold a scalpel in flippers—as, I believe, Benjamin Franklin once said. Benjamin Franklin, by the way, wanted to make the dolphin the national bird of the United States, that is until he was told that the dolphin is an aquatic mammal and not a bird. He tried to cover his faux pas by quickly suggesting the turkey instead. But by that time, everyone else had voted for the eagle, mainly because it was already on the back of the quarter.

But getting back to my original point, dolphins are incredibly intelligent. They have a highly developed cerebellum, are able to learn complex tasks, and have been known to help swimmers in distress. So what do we do to reward this intelligence? We capture dolphins to put in marine shows. (Not the U.S. Marines, but water parks. I don't even know if the U.S. Marines put on shows. Well, there was Gomer Pyle, I guess.) It's kind of like saying, "Boy that Albert Einstein sure is smart. We should have him in a show. I wonder if he would put on a tutu and jump through a ring of fire."

Dolphins are also killed by commercial fishermen. They get caught in the nets that are used to catch tuna. I'll eat tuna, but only if it has that little sticker of the smiling dolphin with a slash through it. This means that the tuna is dolphin free. Actually, I'd like to see that sticker on other things because, frankly, I don't want dolphin in any of my food. I'd like to see that smiley dolphin sticker on Trix, chocolate cake, toothpaste, everything. They're looking for any way to sneak dolphin into our food because they're so abundant.

I was buying some spaghetti sauce and I saw something really frightening on the can: a sticker with a smiling monkey with a slash through it. I thought, "My god, what was in this stuff before?" Has animal testing become so advanced that it's now animal taste-testing?

I rest my case.

I have always loved animals. When I was about eleven years old, I wanted to be a veterinarian. We had a little laundry room downstairs and I made that my office. I'd sit there, take an encyclopedia and copy from it entries about different types of cats. I'd have a separate file for each breed. So, if somebody came to my house and said, "You know, there's no difference between a Siamese and a Burmese cat," I'd reply, "Oh yeah? Come to my office and I'll show you how wrong you are, Mr. Smartypants." Unfortunately nobody ever came to my house and said that. But, if they had, I'd have been ready.

I think I realized, even at an early age, that the real beauty of pets is that they love you unconditionally. All they would like in return is a bit of attention and some food. And, the food doesn't even have to be that good. It could just come out of a can.

I try to save dogs and take them to shelters so that their owners can find them. It's because I have dogs, and I know I'd be devastated if either . . . damn, what are their names? Oh yeah . . . if either Bootsie or Lippy . . . no, not Lippy . . . Muffin. If either Bootsie or Muffin got lost . . . Bootsie is a beautiful Labrador retriever and Muffin is . . . I'm not exactly sure what Muffin is. When I got her at the shelter, they told me that she was part cocker spaniel and part terrier, but I don't think they knew. They were just making conversation. I think she's part . . . rodent. She's got hair like a possum and a snout like an anteater. But, don't get the wrong impression, she's very pretty. She's got off-beat good looks.

I'll see stray dogs wandering in front of houses and they look so sad. I just feel compelled to do something to rescue them. Sometimes it's hard because they're tied on a leash on someone's front lawn, so you've got to untie it. Or worse, they're behind a fence, so you need wire cutters (which I always have in my car) to get them out. "C'mon, girl. I'll rescue you and find your owners."

Just last week I was driving when I saw this skinny looking stray dog out on the street. So I stopped, got out, and tried to coax the dog into my car so that I could take it to a rescue shelter. All these people on the street were staring at me like I was crazy. Well, I'm kind of used to that, so I continued, "Here boy, here Scrappy." When I don't know an animal's name, I always assume that it's Scrappy—even though I've never been right.

Then I saw why people were staring at me. It wasn't a dog, it was a coyote (who oddly enough was called Scrappy). I can only imagine what a disaster it would have been if I had gotten the coyote in my car. I was a little bit embarrassed, but I make mistakes like that often. I remember once, I met a guy while I was camping and we got along great. We were married two years before I realized he was a grizzly bear.

I don't know why I just thought of this, but, when I was a kid—younger than I am today—I had a gerbil. It was such a fun pet to have because it stayed in its little aquarium with wood shavings and a wheel and seemed to be quite content. I could go to school, go out to play as often as I wanted and not feel guilty. I could take it out and play with it and it seemed to enjoy its little outside-the-aquarium excursions. It's a good starter pet for a kid, because it doesn't require a great deal of responsibility. You don't have to take it out on walks; that exercise wheel was a great invention. No other pet gets a little built-in gym. I wonder if they make little Stairmasters for them as well. Gerbils are the most fit of all rodents, I'd have to say.

You sometimes hear that pets eventually begin to look like their owners. I don't think that's true. We have much more of a say in how we look than a pet does. It's pretty sad if we get fashion tips from our dogs and cats. "What's that you've done to your hair? I love it. Oh . . . shedding. I'll try it."

I do dote on my dogs. I care about my dogs so much that I give them some rights that I don't necessarily advocate for all animals. For instance, Bootsie and Muffin have the right to jump up on my furniture. Also, they have the right to wake me up, clutching balls in their mouths, to see if I want to play. These are not rights I would give to a raccoon or a cougar. Though, if a cougar woke me up with a ball in its mouth, I'd probably play with him. You know, just to be safe. But the next night I would make sure all the doors were locked. I'm not crazy.

Also, I don't believe that animals should have the right to vote, but I do allow Bootsie to help me with my absentee ballot. Muffin doesn't care about politics.

It is amazing to me how perceptive pets are and how sensitive they are to their environment. Just look at how they behave before an earthquake. Before the Northridge quake, Bootsie and Muffin were very anxious. They knew it was going to happen. They were in the doorway, telling me to hurry up and join them. Bootsie had grabbed a few cans of food and Muffin had some extra batteries and a little bottle of brandy. They knew.

Though I have dogs now, for most of my life I've had cats as pets. I, personally (in some ways, but not in others), like cats more than dogs (with no offense meant to either Bootsie or Muffin). But have you ever had a cat in heat? They just change on you. Once she was my kitten, my adorable little pet. Then, she's a hooker. I went into the bathroom one night, and she was putting on mascara, "To-night, to-night, won't be just any . . . la la. Hm, hm." She didn't know the whole song. "Hm, hm." She just knew some of the words. "Hm, hm."

She was an indoor cat, but male cats knew she was in there somehow. They were just all around the house and somehow she was sneaking out because one morning I found a stamp on her paw. I wouldn't have noticed, but I had just bought this new black light, and she passed right under it. "Hey! What is that?" I said.

And the male cats, they were sneaky the way they tried to get in to see her. One of them disguised himself as a UPS man. He had the truck, the packages, everything. I said, "I'm not falling for that." The suit was just hanging off of him, his little name tag said "Fluffy." "Oh, right. I will *not* sign here. Scoot!" He went off all mad in that big truck, stripping the gears. They don't know how to drive! Cats.

He came back the next day as a cable repairman. Same outfit, little butt crack hanging out this time. So he fooled me. I let him in. He got me Nickelodeon for free, hooked that up somehow. So now I get to see all the old shows.

Smart cat—I'd like to see his test scores!

ask ellen

or ···

it might look like honey,
it might taste like honey,
and bless my corns,
it might even be honey

To chew is human,
to forgive divine.

During the early 1980s, before I became one of America's most beloved comedians (at least that's what Mom calls me; well, she either calls me that or Senorita Monkeyshines) I earned my keep by writing a column called ASK ELLEN OR DON'T ASK ELLEN, IT'S ENTIRELY UP TO YOU AND ABSOLUTELY NO SKIN OFF MY NOSE EITHER WAY, THOUGH IF YOU EVER EXPECT TO GET AN ANSWER THE LEAST YOU CAN DO IS ASK . . . ELLEN THAT IS." Most papers shortened this to ASK ELLEN since the entire title took up all my allotted space. This column, where people would ask me whatever was on their minds, ran in twenty newspapers, nineteen of which were in the Canadian province of Saskatchewan.

I have received many letters asking me to reprint some of my favorite ASK ELLENs. I have received a whole lot more letters begging me *not* to reprint them. I, however, prefer to dwell on the positive (and get away with not writing something new). So without any further ado (or to be honest with just the cutest little teeny bit of ado) here are some of my favorites. Enjoy!

Dear Ellen,
Hi, I am eight years old. The other day I went to my neighbor's house and asked him if I could borrow his toupee for Show and Tell. He told me, "Go to Heck!" I didn't know what that meant, but it sounded bad. So I told him to Fuck Himself. What is Heck?

Signed, Curious.

Dear Curious,
Many people think that Heck is just a polite way of saying Hell. Those people are as wrong as wrong can

be (and believe me, wrong can be pretty damn wrong). Heck is just to the left of Hell, it's a suburb of Hell. Heck is a little bit nicer than Hell. For instance, Heck has Dairy Queens and you don't have to pay as much for car insurance. People in Hell wish that they were in Heck.

But as nice as Heck might be (and in all honesty, it's not that nice), it is nowhere as good as being in Heaven. Oddly enough, when somebody does something nice, nobody ever says, "Go to Heaven!" I guess that's because a person would have to die before they went to Heaven. Saying "Go to Heaven" is like saying "Drop dead" but with a positive spin.

Dear Ellen,
How would I explain chewing gum to an alien? I'm just curious. There is no alien holding me hostage and making me answer stupid questions. I do not need HELP! Because, if there was an alien and he thought I was asking for HELP!, he might take me to his spacecraft, fly me to his planet, and put me in a zoo.

Signed, PLEASE HELP ME!!

Dear Please Help Me,
Good Question. Chewing gum is an anomaly. I'm not exactly sure what anomaly means, but I'm sure that it could apply to chewing gum. A good rule of thumb is, whenever you don't know the answer to a question, say that it's an anomaly and then run away before anyone can ask you any more questions.

That being said, if I were to explain chewing gum to

your hypothetical alien, I would say, "Well, Mr. or Ms. Alien, chewing gum is something you put in your mouth, but it's not really food. I mean, it has a flavor and everything—at least for a few minutes, then even that goes away—but there are no nutrients in it. It's not even candy. You can swallow candy, but it's probably best that you don't swallow gum. I guess humans buy it because they just love chewing; hence the saying, 'To chew is human, to forgive divine.' "

159

I'm not actually sure if I got that saying 100 percent right. One thing I can tell you about gum, though, is that there is no way of getting it out of your mouth that isn't disgusting. You either have to reach into your mouth with your fingers (and who knows where they've been; I suppose you probably do, unless you've fallen asleep and there's no telling where fingers go when you're sleeping) and yank out the tasteless, saliva-drenched morsel, or you have to spit it out. No matter how much you practice, you can never make spitting out gum look demure.

At some time in your life, you will step on gum that has been spit out on the street. The way to get it off your shoe is to put an ice cube on it. The gum will harden and you can scrape it off with a spatula (see last week's column: 25 REASONS TO CARRY A SPATULA WITH YOU AT ALL TIMES).

Dear Ellen,
If you ran the Academy Awards, how would you change things?

Signed, Just felt like sending a letter

Dear Just . . .
If I ran the Academy Awards (and I'm not saying that I don't, though I'm pretty sure that I don't), I would make them a lot livelier. I would assume that everybody who was nominated equally deserved to win. So, when the nominations are announced, I'd have the Oscar go to the first person from each category to arrive at the location where the announcement came from (it would be a secret and change each year). You could win either by being fast or by preventing the other nominees from getting to the destination (by means of kidnapping, putting under anesthesia, etc). I think it would make for exciting television while still maintaining the dignity of the award.

Dear Ellen,
I read this saying the other day: "To know that we know what we know, and that we do not know what we do not know, that is true knowledge," Henry David Thoreau.
    At first I found this very inspirational, then I realized I had no idea what it meant. What gives?

Signed, Am I an idiot or what?

Dear Am I an idiot or what?
You are not an idiot. Ipso facto you're a what. What's a what you might ask. But, you didn't ask. So I won't tell. Ha, ha.

If you're worried that you don't understand the saying, here is a simpler way of stating it: Knowing that you know that you know what you know is knowledge of that which you know. You know?

Hope that's helpful.

161

Dear Ellen,

I have these friends . . . well, they're not really friends, they're people I work with. I call them friends because it makes my life seem less lonely than if I call them co-workers. Anyway, these very close *friends* of mine are always gossiping. Whenever somebody leaves the room, they begin talking about that person behind his or her back (his if it's a male, hers if it's a female).

I found this very amusing until I figured out something: Hey, when I leave the room, they must be gossiping about me! How can I prevent this from happening?

Signed, Person with lots of friends

Dear Person . . .

The only way you can prevent people from talking about you when you leave the room is to never leave the room. I would recommend this course of action highly. Don't go to lunch. Don't go to the bathroom— wear a catheter if necessary. And always make sure your back is to a wall. Never let anyone sneak up on you. If a phone rings, don't answer it. Follow these simple rules and your workplace will be fun to work in again.

Dear Ellen,
Whenever I'm walking my dog, people bend down and talk to her, saying things like, "You're a cute doggie. How old are you?" Is this weird?

Signed, Wondering if it's weird that people bend down and talk to my dog

Dear Wondering . . .
It's only weird if they're expecting an answer back from your dog.

It would also be weird if somebody asked you how old your dog was and you looked down at her and said, "Say that you're two years old," in the same voice that people talk to babies with. Because no matter how long you pleaded, the dog is never going to talk (neither is the baby, unless you plead for a year or so).

Also, a dog doesn't care how old she is. Yet some people have birthday parties for their dogs. Some people have *surprise* birthday parties for their dogs. That's just a waste, because any party would be a surprise to a dog. She has no idea when her birthday is. A dog doesn't sit around thinking, "Boy, my birthday is coming up in two weeks. I hope they throw me a party."

Dear Ellen,
How would I explain to an alien that people bet on horse races and dog races, but they don't bet on people running or car races?

Please forward your answer to the Municipal 200 on

the planet Qogratz, located on the far side of the Milky Way.

Signed, Going on a trip and don't expect to be back any time soon

Dear Going . . .
I guess in order to bet on a race there has to be some sort of animal involved. We'd probably bet on the Indy 500 if there was a monkey driving around in a race car. Maybe we'd bet on the 100-yard dash if all the sprinters had to carry a pig while they ran (this might make the winning times a lot slower).

   Also, have fun on your trip. I hope that you read this before you leave, because I'm not sure that I can forward this answer; you didn't leave a zip code! You know how strict they are about that.

Dear Ellen,
Hi. My name is Spoogy. What do you think about that?

Signed, Spoogy

Dear Spoogy,
I think it's great.

Dear Ellen,
Who stole the cookies from the cookie jar?

Signed, Spoogy

Dear Spoogy,
You stole the cookies from the cookie jar.

Dear Ellen,
Not me.

Signed, Spoogy

Dear Spoogy,
Yes, you.

Dear Ellen,
Couldn't be.

Signed, Spoogy

Dear Spoogy,
Then who, my dear Spoogy, then who?
    You obviously need more help than I can give. I recommend you talk to a counselor or a clergyman or basically anyone else besides me.

crazy superstitions that really work!

....

If your palms are ringing...

1. If your nose itches, someone wants to kiss you.

2. If the clasp on your necklace has turned to the front, someone is thinking about you.

3. If your ears are burning, someone is talking about you. If your ears are itchy, they are dirty.

4. If your palms are burning, you will be coming into some money soon. If your palms are ringing, you are crazy.

5. If you hit your funny bone, you will hear a joke within twenty-four hours. If you hit your head, you will cry.

6. If you find a bunny in your yard, a distant relative will marry a Finnish diplomat in September.

7. If a spider is in your pants, you will hop around and scream.

8. If you sleep with a teabag tied around your head, I don't know why.

the benefits
of being a
celebrity

by ....

ellen degeneres, big enormous star

What does it feel like
to be a star?

Many people ask me, "Ellen, how has fame changed your life? What does it feel like to be a star?" And really, it makes me laugh—I mean I'm no different from anyone else. I guess just because I'm a "celebrity" (or, if you prefer, America's most beloved comic sweetheart) they assume my life is weird or something. My daily routine is pretty much the same as yours—or even yours.

I wake up around—oh seven, seven o' five. My houseboy, Quaw, prepares my breakfast, usually a Figurine and a glass of apple juice and maybe half of a banana. Then I'll play with my pony for a while out by the lake—that brings me up to lunch time. Quaw will usually surprise me for lunch. Sometimes he'll be dressed up as an Indian and serve some spicy Indian dish and a Pepsi with a straw. Or, he'll be a Spanish conquistador or a Chinese emperor and I'll pretend to be a peasant girl from the village who's hungry and he invites me into the palace for a cup of soup. Then he asks me if I want to use his washroom to bathe, and I do and then at 3 P.M. I'll watch *Oprah*. After that, I'll write a letter to *People* magazine or *US* magazine to compliment or protest some story they wrote about Johnny Depp or Madonna or somebody.

Okay, that brings me to around six o'clock when I go pick up the kids from day care. Not my kids; I drive a van for the neighborhood moms who are busy. Then I'll be home in time for *Wheel of Fortune* and a hot meal: maybe lasagna or pasta with a creamy pesto sauce or some vegetarian burritos.

From 8:30–9:30 Quaw will do some exotic dancing in the disco for me and some of my close friends. Then we will talk and visit and finally head on into the den to the big-screen TV to watch either Jerry Springer, CNN, or whatever is on my outdoor security camera. Around midnight my friends mosey out of my house, I take a couple of Excedrin PMs and a glass of Diet Sprite, and call it a day.

Though my typical day is nothing out of the ordinary, I must begrudgingly admit that being a celebrity does carry with it some pretty cool perks. I'd like to list for you now some benefits of being a celebrity.

"Hey," you might now be interjecting, "I don't have to read the rest of this—I already am a celebrity." Well let's make sure you know what the term *celebrity* means. A celebrity is a well-known famous person who is easily recognized. If you are a person who has chosen not to have sex, you're not a celebrity—you're celibate. Now, I'm sure there are many benefits to being a celibate, though the only two that spring to my mind are: one, you probably become better at other things, like, for instance the Jumble or remembering *Star Trek* trivia; and two, I would imagine you don't have to change your sheets quite so often. But that's not what I care to talk about right now.

Here then are some advantages of being a celebrity.

When you're a celebrity you tend to get special treatment. For instance, I was at the Sizzler yesterday and a woman who worked there came up to me and told me that I could eat all the shrimp I wanted. I heard her say it to a lot of other people, too —which goes to prove one thing: A lot of celebrities eat at the Sizzler.

At the Gap they have a special changing cubicle just for celebrities—it's just like all the others except it has a star on the door and a bowl of fruit inside. Also, you're not limited to three items, you can bring in four.

When a celebrity plays Scrabble, the letters Q and Z are worth twenty points and not ten, the celebrity is allowed to see her opponents' tiles, and whatever a celebrity says is a word is a word (e.g., ZQWXJEM). This may lead to some arguments with your noncelebrity friends, but don't let that worry you. Another benefit to being a celebrity is that you get to win every argument you're in.

In every election, whether it's local, state, or national, a celebrity's vote is counted twice.

One of the major benefits of being a celebrity is that more people know how to pronounce your name correctly. That may not sound like much, but when you have a name like DeGeneres, believe you me, that counts for plenty. An added plus is that more people know how to pronounce my brother's name as well.

The National Board of Health says that celebrities are allowed to eat five eggs a week and not four. If you win a People's Choice Award you're allowed fifteen eggs a week.

Celebrities get free HBO for a week once or twice a year. I know this happens for me; I'm guessing it happens for other celebrities, too.

Though it might be considered pretentious in others, it is never showy for a celebrity to have an entourage. I personally don't go anywhere without an entourage of fifteen to thirty-five people complimenting me incessantly and laughing loudly at all of my jokes. Though it gets kind of crowded when I go into one of those little booths to have my passport picture taken, I find that it's worth the inconvenience. Among the members of my entourage (or if you prefer retinue or gang) are: Stumpy, my personal trainer; Lupé, my sheep herder (I keep her around in case I ever decide to purchase some sheep or even just one sheep); Pantry, the woman who brushes my teeth; Todd, my food taster (I'm sorry, Todd was my first food taster—he died after eating a bad batch of Rice Krispies Treats that I must have undercooked. Dutch, my second food taster is gone, too. He didn't die; I fired him for either looking me in the eyes, using the word "and," or forgetting to start each sentence with "Madame do you wish that I . . ." A celebrity can fire anybody for whatever reason they decide and not be thought of as rude—in fact it's considered to be sort of cute and whimsical.); Bong

Bong, my tennis pro; and a group of people who don't look familiar to me but claim to be my friends.

Celebrities can drive eight thousand miles without changing their oil. Plus, they get a 5 percent discount at participating Jiffy Lubes.

If a celebrity goes to a hospital for a major operation, any plastic surgery the celebrity desires is included for free. Or if you pay to get one lip injected with collagen, you get your second lip injected for free.

The sign NO SHOES NO SHIRT NO SERVICE never applies to celebrities.

At the supermarket, celebrities are allowed to take thirteen items into the ten-items-or-less lane. They can also pay by check if the sign says CASH ONLY. When they buy milk they can add five days to the expiration date.

Celebrities can go on any ride in any amusement park no matter how short they are.

If a celebrity is on a boat that is sinking—the rule becomes celebrities first, then women and children.

So when you're walking down the street and you think you've spotted your favorite celebrity but you want to be sure, just remember this rule of thumb: A horse sweats, a man perspires, a woman glows—but only a celebrity twinkles.

your own
fantasy
conversation
with ellen
degeneres

....

But I think it's you
who are so cool.

I received the cutest letter the other day. Here it is:

Dear Ellen,
How are you? I am fine. I hope you are fine, too. I mean it. You are my most favoritest celebrity in the whole world. I like you even more than that guy in the commercial who talks with a funny voice. (He makes me laugh. Ha Ha Ha!!!)

You seem very nice. I wish that I could meet you so that we could have a nice talk. Here is a picture I've drawn of you and me having a nice talk.

The dog in the picture with me is my dog. His name is Mr. Doggy. I named him. My wife thinks that it's a stupid name. She says that a forty-two-year-old man who works as a High School Vice-Principal should be able to come up with a better name. I think it's a good name.

Yours truly,
Bobby Munchloney

Actually, upon rereading that letter, it's not all that cute. But, it does raise an interesting question: What would it be like to talk with Ellen DeGeneres?

I know that before I became a celebrity I always wondered what it would be like to talk to somebody famous like Carol

Burnett, Stevie Wonder, Elizabeth Taylor, Zamfir, Punch, Judy, or Marlon Brando. Would they be nice, would they be interesting, would they lend me money?

Most of you will never get the chance to talk with me, unfortunately (or fortunately, in the case of Bobby Munchloney). So for your benefit, I've decided to provide you with a fantasy interactive conversation between yourself and myself. All you have to do is fill in your own dialogue in the space provided. My responses are 100 percent my own and exactly what I would say in reaction to whatever you would say.

For the purpose of this little fantasy, your character will be called Complete Stranger (later shortened to CS). I will be Ellen. Even if your name is Ellen, only say the lines you've written for Complete Stranger. Otherwise, we'll have anarchy on our hands. (Anarchy, by the way, is very hard to get off of your hands. Again, you'd think club soda might work, but it doesn't.)

Let the fantasy begin.

SETTING: The housewares section of a large department store.

ACTION: You are browsing, carrying a bag of clothes you just bought, when you see me looking at a selection of fry daddies and electric butter churners. You do a double take and then tentatively approach me.

Suddenly, you are lifted off the ground, your feet dangling in the air like the branches of a banana tree during a monsoon (I'm sorry—I couldn't think of a better simile). Seeing that you mean me no harm, I motion for my 250-pound bodyguard to put you down. He does so in a surprisingly gentle way.

Ellen: Hi, I'm Ellen DeGeneres. Who are you?

Complete Stranger: _____ _____.

Ellen: And what do your friends call you?

C.S.: _____ _____.

Ellen: Wow! That's one of my favorite names. In fact, I have a
goldfish named (your name). You're not my goldfish, are you?   179
Because if you are, I don't think it's safe for you to be out of
the bowl for very long.

C.S.: ___ _____ _____ _____.

Ellen: Well, thank you for saying that. It makes me happy that
you find me very, very funny.

C.S.: ___ _____ _____.

Ellen: I stand corrected, very, very, *very* funny. Say, (your
name), what is it that you do for a living?

C.S.: ____ _____ _____ _____ ____.

Ellen: That is such a coincidence. If I wasn't doing what I'm
doing, I'd want to be a (your job). I even thought of studying
to be a (your job), but everybody said . . .

C.S.: _____ _____, "_____."

Ellen: (Laughing) That's right! That's exactly what everybody
said. I guess being a (your job) makes you really understand
people.

(*Note*: While we're talking I'm looking at you and only you. You
have my complete attention. I'm not staring around bored or

planning some way to escape. I am genuinely interested in what you have to say.)

C.S.: _____ _____ _____.

Ellen: Excuse me, but I think it's you who are so cool. And I can tell that you have a great sense of humor.

C.S.: _____ _____ ___ ___?

Ellen: Sure, I'd love to hear a joke.

C.S.: _____ _____ _____
_____. _____ _____
_____. _____, "_____ _____
_____ _____?" _____ _____
_____. _____, "_____ ___ _____
_____!" _____ (_____) _____.

Ellen: (Laughing hysterically) That's hilarious. I usually don't like dirty jokes, but that was very good. That was a great impersonation, too. I hate to be a bother, but do you know any other jokes?

C.S.: _____ _____ _____?

Ellen: Who's there?

C.S.: _____.

Ellen: Tomato, who?

C.S.: _____ _____ ___ _____ _____
_____ ___ _____ _____ _____.

Ellen: (Laughing even harder than before) That is so clever. I never would have figured that one out in a million years.

C.S.: _____ _____ _____
_____ _____.

Ellen: You are absolutely right. But, I guess I've learned to see through the pain. You are very perceptive. Say, you know about me, I'd like to know about you. What are your dreams, your goals, your philosophy of life? I'd really, really like to know.

C.S.: _____ _____
_____ _____ _____.
_____-_____! _____ _____
_____ _____ _____? _____
_____ _____ {_____} _____
_____. _____ _____
_____ _____ _____.

Ellen: Uh huh.

C.S.: _____ _____ _____. __ _____
_____ _____ ____. _____ _____
_____ _____ _____.

Ellen: Yeah.

C.S.: _____ _____ _____?
_____ _____ _____. _____ _____
_____ _____ _____ _____
_____. _____ _____ _____
_____ _____ _____: _____

_____; _____; _____!!!!!! _____

___ _____ ____ _____ _____

_____ _____ _____ _____.

(*Note:* I'm sure that you'd have a lot more to say, and I'd have let you go on for pages, but my editor insisted that *I* have more words. In his narrow world view, your words don't count toward the 60,000 words that I'm legally bound to provide for this book. And as much as I insisted that (your name) had some bold ideas that people ought to hear, he, obviously, felt otherwise. That's life.)

Ellen: I agree with every word you said. Also, just to change the subject slightly, I think you've got the coolest clothes I've ever seen. I think I'm going to start dressing just like you.

Just then I take a bite out of my sandwich and start choking. By the way, we're both eating sandwiches. You're eating a fried chicken sandwich—unless you're vegetarian; then it can be a cucumber sandwich. If you haven't been eating, I'm afraid you're going to have to go to the beginning of our conversation, grab a sandwich, and start over again. Sorry, rules are rules.

You reach behind me and give me the Heimlich maneuver. A chunk of food flies out of my mouth.

Ellen: You saved my life. For now on in I'm not going to call what you just did the Heimlich maneuver, I'm going to call it the (your name) maneuver. Honest. Is there anything I can do for you?

C.S.: _____ _____ _____?

Ellen: Sure, how much do you need?

C.S.: $___, ___, ___.

Ellen: That's an awful lot of money, but . . . What the hey, you deserve it. Hey, are you thinking what I'm thinking?

C.S.: ___ ___ ___.   183

Ellen: Exactly. Let's go right now. Time's a wasting, my friend.

fin

And that is the end of the fantasy conversation. I hope that you enjoyed it as much as I did. Take care and see you next time.

experiments
in human
behavior

You're just so vulnerable
at that time.

SOME THINGS THAT I HATE IN PEOPLE
Impatience
Intolerance
Infidelity
Insecticides

I don't like to generalize, but you can always tell people's personalities by the cars they drive . . . and the bumper stickers they put on their cars (Sometimes it's no more than pure sexual advertising: "Honk if you're horny." You never see people putting those stickers on their front door: "Knock if you're nasty.") . . . and the clothes they wear . . . and the music they listen to . . . and the way they walk . . . and what they say . . . and what they do. But, once again, that's just a generalization.

Here's what I'm really trying to say: If we don't want to define ourselves by things as superficial as our appearances, we're stuck with the revolting alternative of being judged by our actions, by what we do.

Now there are the big issues of good and evil. (Murder is evil; donating blood is good. If either of these statements is news to you, put down this book, go to the nearest police station, and turn yourself in—they'll know what to do with you there.) However, I'd like to deal with the smaller issues. I want to talk about the things that are neither good nor evil but by which we judge ourselves anyway—the little things we do and the countless situations we find ourselves in that conspire to make us feel like idiots.

Do I feel like an idiot? If I had a nickel for every time I felt like an idiot, I'd be very rich. But I'd be too embarrassed to spend any of what I'm sure I'd refer to as my "idiot money." If I were to spend it, buying an expensive item like a car with about 800,000 nickels would make me feel even more like an idiot.

Though the good news is, I'd get another nickel for doing it. This might be a moot point.

We all feel like idiots at one time or another. Even if we feel we're cool 98 percent of the time, that 2 percent doofus is poised to take over our bodies without any warning. It just takes a crack in the sidewalk—one little trip. We feel like fools, turning back to look at it. "There's a pebble, somebody better put up some orange cones to warn the others. Everybody's gonna trip like I did." Then we look back that one more time to show the pebble who's boss, "Damn pebble, why-I-oughta . . ."

We do that because we think that people are staring at us, sensing our inadequacy, noting our flaws, mocking our clumsiness. But perhaps, sadly (though, for the purpose of this book, perhaps not—perhaps humorously instead), nobody is noticing. Everybody is too busy worrying that they look like idiots to care about you.

If you think that none of this applies to you, just take a look at your picture in your high school yearbook. Because closer to the surface than you think is that awkward adolescent hoping that people like her and praying that nobody notices how much she hopes that people like her and knowing that if people knew what an idiot she was, they'd never like her. Or maybe not. Maybe you'd just see how funny you looked back then and have a good laugh. Either way it's worthwhile.

One activity that can bring out feelings of idiocy is singing. Sometimes it's because you're belting out a tune to yourself (That sounds violent, doesn't it? "You've been a very bad tune. I'm a gonna give you a belting that you won't soon forget!") and you're feeling good—you're sure that you sound just like Whitney Houston. Then you look up and realize that you're not by yourself—people are watching you (if you're in a car or a house with picture windows) and perhaps even hearing you (if you're in a plane, wearing headphones, and listening to "Pop Goes the Country" or "The Now Sound").

Sometimes it's because you're singing with a group of people and you don't know the lyrics to the song. Then you have to play that little game we always play. We mumble through the words we don't know, but then to make up for it, we sing the chorus really, really loud.

We're hoping the others are thinking, "I guess she didn't wanna sing on that little mumbly part back there. Obviously she knows the song—she sang the chorus *really* loud. She is cool."

Have you ever heard somebody sing some lyrics that you've never sung before, and you realize you've never sung the right words in that song? You hear them and all of a sudden you say to yourself, " 'Life in the Fast Lane?' *That's* what they're saying right there? 'Life in the Fast Lane?' " You think, "Why have I been singing 'Wipe in the Vaseline?' How many people have heard me sing 'Wipe in the Vaseline?' " I am an idiot. But it sounds like that, you know?

There are certain songs you just know have parts where there aren't any real lyrics, because nobody can figure them out even after hearing the song over and over and over again. For instance, that Aretha Franklin song "Respect." Everybody gets the part: "R-E-S-P-E-C-T. *Find out what it means to me. R-E-S-P-E-C-T.*" But what follows is anybody's guess. To me it's either *"Da cha, te ee cee tee. Ho!"* or *"Something about a tee-pee. Ho!"* But then everybody is back on board with *"Sock it to me. Sock it to me. Sock it to me."*

Sometimes it's just as embarrassing to get the words to a song right. I think in the seventies we really had some songs that were just idiotic songs, and the lyrics were clear as can be.

Do you remember that song by Three Dog Night, "Joy to the World"? It started off with "Jeremiah was a bullfrog." It was catchy, so you wanted to sing. And then we were hooked, and we were just singing along . . . *"Jeremiah was a bullfrog. Was a good friend of mine. I never understood a single word he said, but I helped him drink his wine."*

Of course that made perfect sense to us. Why should we question that? We've all had friends who were frogs. We didn't fully understand what they were saying, but if it seemed like they wanted you to help them drink some wine, you did it. They would always have some mighty fine wine with 'em, too. Frogs could get ahold of that stuff.

But back to feeling like an idiot. Two places that tend to bring out the "Oh my god, I'm such a nincompoop" in most of us are elevators and public bathrooms. Now, the difference between an elevator and a public bathroom is . . . Wait. If you don't already know the difference between an elevator and a public bathroom, nothing I say is going to be of much help. In the best-case scenario, you're going to be standing in a stall for a long time, wondering why you're not going anywhere. I don't even want to think about the worst-case scenario.

When we're inside an elevator we feel we have to look above us at the floor numbers changing, as if it's by the force of our will that the elevator is rising. If you want to make others in the elevator feel uncomfortable, stay facing the back wall after you enter. The downside of this little gag is that you're pretty likely to miss your floor.

We always do this: we walk up to an elevator, someone's already there, they're waiting, they've pushed the button, the button is lit. We walk up and push the button, thinking, "Obviously you didn't push it correctly. I'll have to push it myself.

Now the elevator will come." Then someone else walks up and they push the button again. Suddenly you're offended. You want to say, "You idiot, I pushed it, he pushed it." Then, to the original pusher, "Can you believe people?"

Or, if you go to the elevator by yourself, you push the button, you wait for the elevator to come, the elevator doesn't come. You push the button six more times. Like that's helping. As if the elevator's thinking, "Oh, a half dozen people are there now. I better hurry. I thought it was just that one woman. I was resting. Oh no, I . . . , I could lose my job! I could become stairs!"

In a public bathroom you're in your own little individual private stall, actually going to the bathroom. For some reason either you forgot to lock the door, or the lock is gone. Suddenly, a perfect stranger opens the door on you. They look at you. You always look at them the same way (sort of a cross between a deer caught in the headlights and a deer caught doing something else, I'm not sure what). They close it immediately and always say, "Oh, I'm sorry." Then we say, "It's okay."

We don't mean this. I think we'd be surprised if they turned around and came back in, actually. "Oh-oh!" "You said it was all right. Hey everybody, come on in! She said it was okay! Get Julie! This is Julie. And you are? There's no need to holler. Let's go, Julie. Yeah, she said it was okay, I wouldn't have just walked in."

It's just so scary if there's no lock on that door; you're so vulnerable at that time. You're scared someone's going to push the door open on you. Imagine if someone had an aerial view of what we looked like in there, trying to keep the door shut. The positions that we have ourselves in. Then we have the *"em-em"* noise, that territory cough that we use. Somehow it scares people away. *"Eeemmmm."*

But, even if there is a lock, there are some people who will continue to try to open the door until you say, "Somebody's in here." What are they thinking? "It's just stuck, I know it. Just somebody's shoes they left in there earlier. Get the ramrod, this one is tight."

Some of the bathrooms are fancy, they have the railings on each side of the toilet, and you might assume that's for the elderly or the handicapped. It's really for people who are paranoid about catching germs—they can balance themselves above the toilet. That iron cross is hard to do, I tell you that. And the dismount! You need a spotter, you do. That's why women go in pairs—"I'm going. Spot me." And when you do an incredible job the judges (you bet there are judges in there) yell, "TEN!"

Sometimes you need those bars, don't you? Sometimes you walk in, the seats are wet. That is a horrible experience. Have you ever just not been thinking, you're in a hurry, you just walk in, you sit, "OH! Eeeesh!!" How does this happen? I mean, what are these women doing in there?

I'm sorry. I got carried away.

I think we do some idiotic things out of habit. Have you ever noticed that whenever you're with someone and you taste something that tastes bad, you always want the person with you to taste it immediately?

"That was disgusting, taste it. Taste it, it's gross. Taste how bad it is." And they always do.

Or, do you ever run out of room on the front of the letter you're writing then write "Over" on the bottom of the letter? We're not giving the person getting the letter much credit. It's not like if it wasn't there, they'd get to the bottom of the page, ". . . and so Kathy and I went shopping and we— Now that's the craziest thing. I don't know why she just ended that way. I hope nothing happened to her. She managed to seal the envelope. She must have gotten it to a mailbox somehow."

"Could it be this way? On the back? Never mind, don't call her, I found it. It was on the back. I followed the arrow."

193

Sometimes I feel like an idiot when I'm with people who have more power than me. I don't mean someone like Hercules (though he probably would make me feel uncomfortable; the age difference alone—a few thousand years, I'm guessing— would make it hard for us to find things in common to talk about), I mean someone who has power over me. I mean policemen. I mean policemen who pull me over when I've been speeding.

I get nervous, so I try to lighten things up by using humor. And you know what? I'm always amazed that people (and by people I mean policemen) don't have the same sense of humor that I do.

For instance, I was pulled over in Los Angeles last week. I was driving—I was speeding. It was obvious I was speeding; I was going very, very fast. So, this policeman pulls me over. He comes up to the window of the car and says, "You know why I pulled you over?" And so I said, "Because of the dead bodies in the trunk?" To make a long story short, he didn't see the comedy in my remark. Like I said, no sense of humor.

Do you ever lie to a policeman when you get pulled over for speeding? If you look real good that day, you might think you can flirt your way out of the ticket. But, unfortunately, we usually don't dress anticipating a traffic ticket. We're usually wearing some horrible outfit that we just threw on to go out and buy some Häagen-Dazs ice cream. But, we try flirting anyway, and nine times out of ten we end up feeling like idiots (the tenth time we feel even worse).

"Hi, I think Nehru jackets are sexy—don't you, officer? HA, HA, HA. Well, anyway, listen—you know what happened? And I think you'll find this funny—well, not funny, but, well . . . Anyway, okay, I was in my house and I got a phone call from my mother. She said, 'Ellen honey.' That's what she calls me. Well, that's my name—not the honey part—Ellen. Honey's just an endearing term. You can call me Ellen Honey. Anyway, she asked me to 'rush' over—that's the word she used, 'rush.' I said are you okay? She just said, 'Hurry, *please*, hurry.' That's what she said, 'Hurry, please.' Well, you heard what she said. Well, you didn't hear her, but you heard me saying what she said. Anyway, I just hung up. I said 'Okay, bye.' First I said okay, bye, then I hung up really fast and threw this horrible outfit on—because I was naked—doing some aerobics. I like to keep in shape. I'm single so I feel it's important to look my best for men because that's my job as a woman to look good. Because that's important, being single and a woman. I date a lot of guys; I'm not seeing anyone seriously at this particular time, not that I just go out with anyone—that would be trampy—I have to know a person fairly well first before I would go out and I don't think it should always be the man that pays for the dates. I find it's hard to meet decent people. Well, I'm shy—normally. You're easy to talk to though. I don't know what it is about you, there's something very special, unique. I can't quite put my finger on it. Anyway, woo, it's hot today, isn't it?"

Then you bat your eyelashes in what you hope is a sexy way. Then the policeman hands you the ticket and drives away. Then you feel like an idiot for the rest of the day.

Another thing that we do that can make us feel like we're not only idiots, but crazy idiots to boot (to boot is human, to forgive divine) is talk to ourselves. It's hard to walk down the street these days without hearing somebody talking to themselves. In fact, it's safe to assume that anybody you see walking down the street is talking to themselves. Sometimes people walk in groups of two or more to disguise that they're each having their own individual conversations, but they don't fool me.

"You crazy people are talking to yourselves!" I yell out at them.

But, trapped in their own tiny little worlds, they never hear me. Or maybe they don't hear me because I'm in my car with the windows rolled up. Either way, it's safe to say that something is going on.

Though most people engage in what scientists call "Talkee to Selfee," I never talk to myself.

"Oh, yes I do."
"Oh, no I don't."
"Oh, yes I do."
"Oh, no I don't."
"Oh, yes I do."
"Oh, no I don't."

Author's Note: This conversation was supposed to go on for another ninety pages, and in my mind would have gotten funnier and funnier (I swear, after fifty pages you would have just been screaming with laughter) and, at the same time, fulfilled my obligation to turn in a book of at least 60,000 words.

My editor tried to convince me that this wasn't a good idea. I said, "Is too." He said, "Is not." I said, "Is too." He then said he wasn't going to fall into that trap and that furthermore, none of those words would be counted in the 60,000 that I owe him.

"Why?" I asked. He replied something that to my ear sounded like, "Blah blah blah blah blah blah blah blah blah blah

blah blah blah blah blah blah blah blah blah blah blah blah blah blah blah blah blah blah blah blah blah blah blah blah blah blah blah blah blah blah blah blah blah blah blah . . ." This would have gone on most humorously, but my cold-hearted editor said he wouldn't count any of the blahs as words either.

Finally, when my editor was unable to convince me to change what I saw as my personal vision of what this book should be, my editor's lawyers tried a different approach— something about breach of contract and wanting their money back, I think. Well, we all had a good laugh, after which I completely caved in.

So back to the story, which, in case you forgot, is about talking to yourself.

"Oh, yes I do."
"Oh, no I don't. Hey, go behind that door."
"Okay." *SLAM!!!!* "Hey, you fooled me. Let me back in."
"No, I've got a book to write. Leave me alone."
"Okay. Sorry. Good-bye."

Now where was I? Oh, right. Though most people do talk to themselves, a lot of people don't. But don't get me wrong, they would like to learn how. So, for their benefit, I thought I'd jot down a few words on how they can join the majority and learn the art of self-conversation.

The main advantage of talking to yourself is that sometimes you're the only person who wants to talk to you. Unfortunately this could be because you are extremely boring. If that's the case, then talking to yourself can be a benefit to both you and the outside world—sparing others the expense of listening to you and your mundane ramblings.

Other times, you are the only person available to talk with. Maybe you're in solitary confinement or stranded on a desert isle or, in the worst-case scenario, mistakenly buried alive. But, luckily for you, you've been buried alive with this book—even though it may be difficult to turn the pages. Also, the lighting probably isn't that good. Then again, when you're buried alive, eye strain is probably the least of your worries.

Some people need a crutch in learning to talk to them- selves, so they talk to their television sets first. If for some reason you feel that talking to a TV is less insane than talking to yourself, then more power to you. If you're not sure how to begin talking to your TV, here are a few sample starter phrases:

"Oh boy, this is going to be fun fun funny."

"Look out behind you!"

"I think you're lying. I don't think it's going to rain tomorrow. What do you say about them apples, Mr. Weatherman?"

"Oh yeah, laugh while you got the chance, you criminal scum. Because I got the feeling that in a few minutes that laugh is gonna be wiped off your face by Barnaby Jones, P.I."

After you've gotten the hang of talking to your television you can begin the weaning process by moving on to talking to your radio. If you already sing along with your radio, this will be especially easy for you, though you may want to switch from a music station to talk radio—which, I should note, was specifically designed for people who talk to themselves. If you already sing along to talk radio, well . . . I don't know what to say. You're on your own.

From there on, the weaning process will be easier and easier for you. You've already moved from talking to your TV to talking to your radio. You follow this by talking to your toaster ("Oh yes, make it brown and crisp, just the way I like it."), then to your toast, then your pen, then your pencil, then your eraser, then you talk to a tiny piece of lint in your pocket, and finally you're ready, willing, and able to talk to yourself.

Remember, a person who talks to herself is a healthy person. There's nothing wrong with it. In fact, there was a survey done on people who talk to themselves. . . .

"No, there wasn't."

"Yes, there was. Hey, how did I get back in here?"

"I had a key to the door, ha ha ha."

"The survey said that 90 percent of all people talk to themselves."

"I'm crazy. I'm just making that up.

"Oh, no I'm not. I read it; it's healthy."

"I'm just saying that because I want to feel better about myself."

I'm sorry, but I'm going to have to stop right here. I and myself have an appointment to go to couples therapy to try to work out some of these issues. In the meantime, good luck in talking to yourselves.

ellen's sure-fire cures for the things that ail ye

For a headache...

Contrary to what you may have heard, I am not a doctor. I do not play a doctor on TV (if you think that I do, then you either have some sort of attention disorder or you've been watching the wrong show). I have not even played "Doctor" for a very long time—at least fifteen years . . . okay, ten.

I do not own a stethoscope. Your medical insurance, no matter how good, will never cover anything that I do. If you were to see me on the street and yell out, "Hey, Doc, how's it going?" I would walk away without responding (thinking to myself that you either mistook me for somebody else or were potentially dangerous). I can not legally prescribe drugs.

I have no medical training whatsoever. Since I was raised a Christian Scientist, in high school I was excused from all science classes; I wasn't supposed to learn about the human body. On the plus side, I never had to dissect a frog. (I don't see why anybody has to dissect a frog these days; I know I'd be upset if a giant frog came to earth and decided that he wanted to dissect humans, and I bet that nine out of ten Americans would agree with me in regard to the giant frog. The tenth guy . . . well, he's the kind of person that, if you happen to see him walking down the street, it's probably best that you avoid eye contact.)

The negative side of being excused from all those science classes was that for the longest time I didn't know anything about the human body at all. When my stomach hurt, I said I had a stomach*cake*—I didn't know it was stomachache. While that sort of mistake is cute in a four-year-old, in a teenager it raises a few eyebrows. There are still parts of the human body that I'm just learning about now (internal parts—I know the outside really well; I know my hands, my legs, those ten little things at the end of my feet, and everything else).

All that being said, despite my lack of even the flimsiest credential, I have some advice on how to cure some common ailments that might bother you. I know nothing about nothing, but these are things that have either worked for me occasionally, or things that I've never tried, but feel strongly enough will work nonetheless. I think that you're going to find them extremely useful.

Hiccups

We get hiccups when our esophagus and trachea get into a fight over who is better friends with the gallbladder. When you divide the word *hiccups* into two parts, you get hic and cups. If there is any significance to that, scientists have yet to find it— though, to be fair to scientists, they're probably not looking very hard.

CURES FOR HICCUPS

While holding your breath (or the breath of the person standing next to you), swallow three thousand times. Immediately shampoo your hair, but don't use conditioner. Repeat.

Hold a kitten on your lap and pet it gently on its little head while singing any song by Air Supply (except from their first album).

With your head bent to a thirty-five-degree angle, bite on a slice of lemon with one eye open and the other closed. If you have an additional eye, do whatever you want with it (your eye, not the lemon).

Start hopping for approximately five minutes, scream as loud as you can, "Hey Mr. Tally Man, tally me bananas!" then do a backward flip. This should only be done if you have plenty of room.

Wearing nothing but a Viking helmet and snowshoes, watch reruns of *Dynasty*.

Call up Tokyo and order Moo Goo Gai Pan. When the delivery man comes, tip him generously. If you live in Tokyo, then call up Belgium and order anything except sweet potatoes.

The Common Cold

Research shows that the common cold is not as common as most people think it is—it's even more so!! It's so common you wouldn't be out of line to call it a floozy. A lot of so-called experts have a lot of so-called cures for the so-called common (so-called) cold. Mine are better. And I should know; I'll have had my current cold for three years this March.

203

CURES FOR THE COMMON COLD

Starve a cold, feed a fever. Punch a cold in the stomach, kick a fever in its ass. Strangle a cold, tickle a fever with an ostrich feather. Throw toilet paper at a cold's house, make a fever sit on a whoopie cushion.

In treating a cold remember the three C's: Cheese, Cheese, and Cottage Cheese (actually those are four C's).

While sitting in an icy, cold bath, smoke a carton of menthol cigarettes and eat plenty of—you guessed it—cheese.

Only eat solids, avoid all fluids (except for liquid cheese).

Steal the bedding from a hospital, wrap yourself in it, and pretend to be The Mummy.

Drive your car while sitting in the passenger seat. Oh, did I tell you, I put a bomb in your car, and it will go off if you drive under fifty miles an hour. What do you do? What do you do?

With unwashed hands, touch your eyes, nose, ears, tongue, and throat as many times as you can in one minute.

Tease your neighbor's hamster. If your neighbor doesn't have a hamster, then tease your neighbor's ferret.

Walking Pneumonia

I don't know who had the bright idea of teaching pneumonia how to walk, but I'd like to find that dunderhead before he decides he wants to teach it how to drive. Some people don't know how to leave well enough alone. I'm not trying to imply

that regular pneumonia is "well enough," I'm just saying . . .
Well, I'm sure you know what I mean.

CURES FOR WALKING PNEUMONIA
Sit down!

Headaches

A lot of people will tell you that if you have a headache, you
should take an aspirin or some other type of pain reliever. What
they don't tell you is that aspirin and its pals cost money. You
have to invest something like two dollars. Sure, my book is
$19.95, but look what else you're getting . . . Okay, let's get
past the money and change the subject.

A lot of people will tell you that if you have a headache you
should pinch that little flap of skin between your thumb and
forefinger. What they don't tell you is maybe you don't feel like
pinching that flap, or maybe you've been dieting so you don't
even have a flap anymore. I'll tell you one thing. I wish I had
never written this paragraph, because now I'm starting to get a
headache.

CURES FOR A HEADACHE
Pummel a bag of chattering teeth, rubber chickens, and other
joke items with a shillelagh. If you don't own a shillelagh, then
either borrow one from a policeman or rent one.

Set your clothes dryer for an hour, sit on top, and "ride 'em
cowboy!"

Pinch the flap between your neck and your waist.

When your neighbors aren't home, sneak into their house,
fix yourself a drink, then see if they have anything weird in
their closets. If they're gone long, take a nap on their new
couch.

Eat pancakes and keep eating them until your headache goes away.

Go to the nearest high school and take the SATs again.

Pretend to be Swedish for a whole day. This might not cure your headache, but it's bound to be a lot of fun, by yimminy.

Sit as close to your television as you possibly can and watch any Ernest movie. Either that or go to an ABBA concert. It's your choice.

I think that I have proved conclusively that I am not in any way, shape, or form in the medical profession. If you persist in thinking otherwise, then there is a good chance that you are, if not completely insane, more than halfway there. And don't go giving me any of that "Laughter is the best medicine" business. If I get strep throat, I'd much rather take penicillin than watch a lot of Benny Hill reruns.

the last chapter

The lawyers have reminded
me that the book must be
at least 60,000 words.

I really feel that this is a complete, well-rounded, fleshed-out piece of work—an eclectic book. A little something for everyone in the family to enjoy. And if it were up to me, I'd say "The End," but it seems that contractually I have not fulfilled my duty —the lawyers have reminded me that the book must be at least 60,000—that's *sixty thousand*—words.

"Wow," you say. Or maybe not—maybe some of you said "wow" or simply thought it in your head. Those of you who did not react at all surely have no concept of the pressure to write that many words, for that is a *whole* lot of words.

In conclusion (and, just between you and me, in order to get the law off my back), I'd like to say a few things that perhaps I neglected or merely didn't expand on or go into detail about. For instance, I have enjoyed writing this book over the past year. It's been a learning experience that I shall never forget. My one regret is that I don't know how to type so I did not use a computer. I have written the entire book in longhand, and I'm not positive, but I believe my right arm is now considerably larger than the left—because I am right-handed.

Sometimes I think much faster than I write, therefore . . . Hey, is *therefore* one word or two? I think it should be two even if it's one word because it is actually two words joined together— it's certainly long enough to be counted as two words. Anyway, sometimes I've misspelled words because I can't write as fast as I think, and I have worried that my publisher will think I am stupid—although spelling should not represent the level of intelligence of a human being.

I prefer to use the term *human being* not because it is two words, but because I like it better than person—that is just my personal taste. I do use the word *person* as well, but I just sometimes prefer *human being*. What does that mean, anyway? I understand saying he is a human—but a *human being*? I also enjoy using the words *homo sapiens*, from time to time. It's funny how many words there are for people (see, there's another one right there). *People* is a term or word used for more than one person. But still we say, "There were a whole bunch of people." Why? You know what I'm saying: if people is already plural, why do we need to say a whole bunch? I'm not saying you, the reader, do that. But surely some people do. I know I have used the phrase before many times.

I just glanced out the window—what a beautiful day it is today. It's so clear I can see the mountains. I live in the Hollywood Hills, and sometimes Los Angeles is so smoggy that I can't see the mountains. But today it's so clear I can see them.

I'm sitting at my desk with my computer next to me—almost mocking me. I do have a computer to store all of my writing on disk. I just type so slowly that I can't write this book on it. I rarely sit at my desk and write. I have written most of this book on airplanes, in hotel rooms, in coffeehouses, in bed, in the kitchen—everywhere but at my desk. Sitting at a desk reminds me too much of school. I hated school. I'm so glad to be out. But when I look back on it, I wish I had paid attention more, studied, learned a lot more. So if you're reading this and you're still in school, don't do what I did. You go ahead and enjoy this time in your life; it only happens once. Knowledge is power and you need power in this world. You need as many advantages as you can get.

There are two little birds outside my window—I'm not sure what kind they are—and to be perfectly honest (and I have been all throughout my book, so why stop now), I don't really care. I believe them to be blue jays—they are "talking" to each other. One will skwawk or squawk or however you spell it, then his pal will respond. It's quite obnoxious and makes it hard for me to concentrate on my poignant writing.

I do wonder what the commotion is all about. What on earth could they be arguing about? Is it possible that they are lovers and in a lovers' quarrel? Did one bird flirt with another bird and the other bird found out? I'm sure that must happen—don't you think so? If you care to respond send all letters to Bantam. Because if it weren't for this 60,000-word clause, I would have been finished and I would not have gone this far and I wouldn't have been sitting here being disturbed by these loud birds. So, it's all their fault, really. 211

Well, I think I am just about to reach my quota, so thank you for hanging in there with me. (If some of you stopped on the last chapter, it's okay because that is really where my book ended—this is just for the lawyers.) But if people stopped reading it—then who am I writing to? No one will ever know that I am telling them it's okay to have stopped there.

I am sitting here writing to myself and to the lawyers. Maybe I should say something to them because I know they are reading. "Hello, lawyers. How are you?" Hey, maybe they aren't reading, they're just counting the words. In that case, I don't even have to form sentences. I can make up total nonsense. Nothing has to mean anything; I can just look around and write down everything I'm looking at or thinking about and no one will ever know. Fireplace, firewood, candles, pictures, lamp, vase, tulips, clock, television, rug, bed, computer, printer, dog, telephone, monitor, books, globe, chair, hats, shoes.

THE END

Phew!